GEORGE THALBEN-BALL

GEORGE THALBEN-BALL

JONATHAN RENNERT

Foreword by Malcolm Williamson, CBE
Master of the Queen's Music

DAVID & CHARLES
Newton Abbot   London   North Pomfret (Vt)

British Library Cataloguing in Publication Data
Rennert, Jonathan
  George Thalben-Ball.
  1. Thalben-Ball, George 2. Organists -
  Biography
  786.5′092′4   ML416.T/
  ISBN 0-7153-7863-5

Library of Congress Catalog Card Number: 79–53736

Typeset by Trade Linotype Ltd, Birmingham
and printed in Great Britain
by Biddles Limited, Guildford
for David & Charles (Publishers) Limited
Brunel House   Newton Abbot   Devon

Published in the United States of America
by David & Charles Inc
North Pomfret   Vermont 05053   USA

CONTENTS

Preface		7
Foreword by Malcolm Williamson, CBE, *Master of the Queen's Music*		13
1	Childhood and early training	15
2	The monster of Muswell Hill	33
3	Music in wartime	42
4	Walford Davies and the Temple	51
5	Master Lough	61
6	Teacher and father	64
7	Melodies of Christendom	70
8	ABC of organists	74
9	Second World War	89
10	At the BBC	94
11	The Temple Psalter	100
12	'A cry of fear': thoughts on organ playing	103
13	The Temple restoration	106
14	'Birmingham makes me practise'	112
15	The Royal Albert Hall	119
16	'I tout I taw a puddy-tat'	121
17	The musical perfectionist	128
18	'Sing with your ears'	133

19 Looking ahead   142

Appendix I: Discography   151

Appendix II: Organ specifications   157

Appendix III: Summary of important dates   169

Appendix IV: The Temple Music Trust   173

Index   174

PREFACE

When Dr Thalben-Ball was first approached with the suggestion of a biography, his reply was simple: 'No-one would want to read about *my* life. No, there are many other people you ought to approach.' It took eighteen months of persuasion before he yielded to the idea, and it fell to me – a long-time and unashamed admirer – to tackle the project.

My first session with this almost legendary figure took place in his London flat, on the top floor of an elegant early-eighteenth-century block known as Paper Buildings in the Inner Temple. The Temple lands form what amounts to a walled city between Fleet Street and the Thames Embankment, in looks not unlike an Oxbridge college. Here, protected by their own police and fire services, live and work two self-governing communities of lawyers, the Honourable Societies of the Inner Temple and the Middle Temple. They own many fine buildings, including a twelfth-century church, and it is here that Dr Thalben-Ball has served for more than sixty years as Organist and Director of the Choir. Furthermore, he is a Master of the Bench of the Inner Temple; in other words he sits, as one of the 'elders' of the society, alongside some of England's leading judges.

I climbed the seventy-four steps to his flat (there is no lift) and, standing breathlessly at the top, marvelled that a man who passed normal retirement age some years ago should live up here. 'As a matter of fact, that's what's kept my heart in good condition,' he confided, 'climbing those stairs three or four times a day.'

At a distance he can look uncompromising, even severe. But 'Doctor', as he is fondly known by his choir and many of his followers, melts in conversation: the universally admired but unapproachable master virtuoso becomes a kindly, unassuming gentleman, telling stories against himself and showing concern for everybody around him. Although he could never quite believe that his life was important enough to be recorded, he went to endless trouble to help me with the book. He searched his memory for facts and anecdotes, and carefully read and criticised drafts of the text.

I was able to follow him in his busy schedule giving weekly concerts in Birmingham Town Hall, 'opening' new and rebuilt organs throughout the United Kingdom, and even in a transatlantic celebrity recital tour. This was inspiring enough. But perhaps most dear to me are memories of choir practices and services in the Temple Church, whose unique atmosphere I try to describe later on in the book.

Many people have assisted me in various ways, from Temple choristers who posed for pictures and devised some ingenious titles for this volume (unfortunately not in the end used) to the staff of such institutions as the General Register Office and the Public Record Office, London, Westminster City Libraries, Kensington and Chelsea Libraries, Haringey Libraries, the British Library and Highgate Cemetery.

I must thank in particular those acquaintances of Dr Thalben-Ball who were kind enough to read a draft of the book: **Ernest Lough**, who has been associated with GTB and the Temple choir as chorister, as juvenile recording artist and as adult singer since the 1920s; **David Lewer**, another former Temple chorister who rejoined the choir as a 'gentleman', whose book on the Temple Church and its music provided me with much background material, and whose practical suggestions resulted in a number of necessary alterations; **Ruth Holmes**, a former pupil and long-time friend; **Colin Goulden**, former President of The Organ Club, who has often turned pages for GTB at recitals; **Joy Upton-Hunn**, whose knowledge of the BBC's religious department was invaluable; **Alan Learmouth**, whose shrewd observations drew on his experience as a publisher; and **François Prins**, who not only read the book, but devoted considerable time and energy over a period of two years to the compilation of its illustrations: rephotographing old prints, taking new pictures and contributing many interesting ideas. I was also able to take advantage of the expertise of my parents: both my journalist father and my novelist mother made constructive comments.

One of the author's 'perks' was the opportunity to speak about GTB with leading members of the musical profession who had worked with him. One such was **Dr Herbert Howells**, who went to some trouble to recount incidents from their sixty-year friendship, which began at the Royal College of Music when both were composition pupils of Sir Charles Stanford. Others were **Sir Adrian Boult** and **Sir William McKie**, the latter, like GTB, an Australian by birth, though when I spoke to him he had retired to Ottawa in Canada from his position as Organist of Westminster Abbey. One great disappointment was that **Dr Harold Darke** died shortly before I was able to arrange an interview.

'Doctor's' pupils have been keen to show their respect for their teacher by contributing memories and advice. **Dr Sydney Watson**, formerly Organist of Christ Church, Oxford, was one of GTB's first students, together with the composer **Dr Gordon Jacob** and the singer and former Director of the Royal College of Music, **Sir Keith Falkner**. All three remember him as a piano professor and a concert pianist – an aspect of his many achievements often forgotten by those who have only seen him at an organ console.

Among his younger pupils, **Dr Kenneth Abbott** (Organist of the City Temple, London – not to be confused with the Temple Church), **Gordon Atkinson** (now living in London, Ontario, where he was President of the Royal Canadian College of Organists), **Margaret Cobb** (formerly Organist of St Margaret's, Lothbury), **James Dalton** (Organist of The Queen's College, Oxford), **Stephen Duro** (now giving recitals under the name Stephen Howard), **Peter Goodman** (City Organist, Kingston-upon-Hull), **Paul Murray** (Music Consultant to the Department of Education, Nova Scotia, Canada), **Jean Trevelyan** (now working with her husband John Churchill in Carleton University, Ottawa, Canada) and **Alan Willmore** (the composer and organist) have all sung GTB's praises, though not without perceptive criticism.

Sydney Ball (George's brother) and his wife **Pauline** showed me great hospitality when I visited them in Eastbourne, and both they and GTB's son **John** showed the same warmth and kindness as does their distinguished relative.

And I must mention my publishers: especially **David St John Thomas** who has a personal interest in the organ world, and **Frances Head**, who has edited the book with such patient thoroughness.

I could continue almost indefinitely. There follows an alphabetical list of some of the other individuals who have given me help and advice during the preparation of this book:

Felix Aprahamian, the writer and authority on the organ world; **Philip Bailey**, formerly Organist of St James's Church, Gunnersbury, London; **John Barrow** of the Royal School of Church Music; **James Beall** of Ottawa, Canada, whose knowledge of English literature proved invaluable; **Jim Berrow** of ATV, Birmingham; **Denise Boon**, from the music library in the University of Birmingham; **Sir John Dykes Bower**, formerly Organist of St Paul's Cathedral, London; **David J. Bowman**, who allowed me to browse through his extensive collection of '78' gramophone records; **W. W. S. Breem**, the Librarian of the Inner Temple; **Harold Britton**, Walsall Borough Organist; **John Busbridge**, of the Royal National Institute for the Blind; **Stephen Cleobury**, Master of Music, Westminster Cathedral; **Alan Crabtree**, formerly Secretary of the Ottawa Centre of the Royal Canadian College of Organists; **Lionel Dakers,** Director of the Royal School of Church Music; **Oliver Davies**, whose official title at the Royal College of Music is Keeper of the Portraits and Ephemera; **J. H. Dermit,** Clerk of the Chamberlain's Court in the City of London's Guildhall; **Ralph Downes,** Organist Emeritus of the Oratory, Brompton, London, and the man whose vision led to the creation of the Royal Festival Hall organ; **The Right Reverend and Right Honourable Gerald Ellison**, Bishop of London; **Susan Farrow**, Organist, Church of Our Lady & St Philip Neri, Sydenham, London; **The Reverend Eric Fenn**, formerly Assistant Director, BBC Religious Broadcasting; **Lilian Forsyth**, Organist and Choir Director, Knox Presbyterian Church, Ottawa, Canada; **Frank Fowler,** Managing Director of the organ-builders William Hill & Son and Norman & Beard Ltd; **Lt-Col Sir Martin Gilliat,** Private Secretary to Her Majesty Queen Elizabeth The Queen Mother; **Dr George Guest,** President of the Royal College of Organists, and Organist of St John's College, Cambridge; **Trevor Harvey**, conductor and writer; **The Reverend Charles Heard**, Vicar of Holy Trinity, Castelnau, Barnes, London, and **Mrs Heard**; **Margaret Henderson** of London; **Christopher Herrick**, Sub-Organist, Westminster Abbey; **Marion Herrod**, Secretary and Lettings Manager of the Royal Albert Hall, London; **Stuart Hibberd**, the one-time BBC announcer; **Colin Horsley**, the pianist; **Carys Hughes**, the Welsh organ recitalist; **Judge Christmas Humphreys** of the Inner Temple; **Dennis Hunt**, Organist of St Mary Magdalene, Paddington, London; **Peter Hurford**, formerly Master of the Music in the Cathedral and Abbey Church of St Alban;

Major David Imlay, Bursar of the Royal College of Music; **Dr Francis Jackson**, Organist of York Minster; **Kenneth James**, tonal consultant with the organ-builders Harrison & Harrison Ltd, and **Mrs James**; **Michael James**, the Assistant Organist of Wimborne Minster and formerly head chorister in the Temple Church; **Tom H. Jeffery** of Dartford, Kent, who has built a unique collection of private recordings of the Temple Church choir; **Duncan Johnston**, Librarian of the Royal College of Organists; **Sir John Johnston**, formerly British High Commissioner in Canada, and **Lady Johnston**; **D. J. Kelly**, Official Secretary at the New South Wales Government Offices in London; **The Reverend Prebendary W. D. Kennedy-Bell**, Reader of the Temple; **Donald F. Lea**, singer, as a boy and man, in the Temple Church choir since 1922; **Ian le Grice**, Organist of St Giles', Cripplegate, London, and formerly a Temple Church chorister; **Simon Lindley,** Master of the Music, Leeds Parish Church, and City Organist, Leeds; **The Reverend Sydney Linton**, formerly Vicar of Holy Trinity, Castelnau, Barnes, London; **Ian Low**, Treasurer, BBC Club Organ Society; **Barry Lyndon**, Clerk of the Royal College of Organists, who allowed himself to be used as a constant source of reference for confirmation of detail; **Michael MacKenzie**, European representative of the American concert organists' agency, Arts Image Ltd; **Lyn McLarin**, the American flautist; **E. McNeill**, Librarian and Keeper of the Records, Middle Temple; **Thod S. Madsen**, General Sales Manager of the Rodgers Organ Company, USA; **Colin Menzies**, President of The Organ Club; **The Very Reverend R. L. P. Milburn**, Master of the Temple; **Adrian Mumford**, Organist of St Anne's, Kew Green, and Treasurer of The Organ Club; **Mrs C. T. Norman-Butler**, Appeal Organiser, Temple Music Trust; **Martin Parr**, formerly Governor of Equatoria and an Alderman on London County Council – a familiar figure in the Temple Church; **Leslie R. Patterson**, owner of a wide-ranging collection of organ miscellany; **Dr Charles Peaker**, the leading Canadian organ recitalist and former Organist of St Paul's, Toronto; **Robert Ponsonby**, Controller of Music, British Broadcasting Corporation; **Richard Popplewell**, formerly Organist of St Michael's, Cornhill, London, where he succeeded Dr Harold Darke, and now Organist, Choirmaster and Composer to Her Majesty's Chapels Royal; **John Prewer**, who has for more than forty years sung bass in the Temple Church choir;

Kevin Reeves of Ottawa, Canada, whose excellent caricature of GTB unfortunately had to be omitted from this volume; **Andrew Rance** of the Royal Academy of Music; **Felicity Rennert**, who named a whippet puppy after Dr Thalben-Ball; **David Robinson**, Organist of St Philip's, Earl's Court, London, and Academic Tutor at the Royal Academy of Music; **Barry Rose**, Master of the Choir, St Paul's Cathedral, London, and GTB's successor as Music Adviser to BBC Religious Broadcasting; **P. L. R. Rowe**, of Westerham, Kent; **Dr Watkins Shaw**, Keeper of the Parry Room library, Royal College of Music; **Justin Sillman** of William Hill & Son and Norman & Beard Ltd; **Robert Smith** of Hornsey Reference Library, London; **Michael Smythe** of Vista Recordings; **John Springford**, British Council Representative in Canada, and **Mrs Springford**; **Colin Stewart** of London; **Frederic Symonds**, General Secretary of The Organ Club and European representative of Arts Image Ltd; **Canon Cyril Taylor**, formerly Assistant to the Head of Religious Broadcasting at the BBC; **Geoffrey Thorpe** of Birmingham Town Hall; **Roger Tucker**, Chairman, BBC Club Organ Society; **John Wallen**, Assistant Bursar of the Royal College of Music; **David de Warrenne**, formerly a treble, now a countertenor, in the Temple Church choir; **Vincent Waterhouse**, Secretary and Chief Administrative Officer, Royal School of Church Music; **Nicholas Webber**, composer and critic; **Sir David Willcocks**, Director of the Royal College of Music; **The Reverend John G. Williams**, formerly Assistant to the Head of Religious Broadcasting at the BBC; and **Dr Malcolm Williamson**, Master of the Queen's Music.

Jonathan Rennert, 1979

FOREWORD

By Malcolm Williamson, CBE, Master of the Queen's Music

The many-sided gifts of George Thalben-Ball are considerable enough to have affected musicians and laymen deeply right across the world. Many know only a few facets of the great man's work in music, and therefore Jonathan Rennert's fresh and vivid biography will give an eye-opening picture of the whole man. For those who have been enriched by his music-making at the Temple Church, or those who have enjoyed his breathtaking organ recitals, it will be a happy revelation to know of the man's optimism and wit; and for those who know it all, an edifying experience to retrace in these pages a career packed with rich and diverse musical experiences. Dr Thalben-Ball is an era of music, musical performance and practical teaching rolled up into one genial and profoundly lovable person.

My first acquaintance with George Thalben-Ball's music-making was from his recordings from the Temple Church, which I loved as an Australian child. Years later, when I met the man, I was delighted to know that I had been born in the same part of Sydney. We were both playing in a tribute recital for Guy Weitz at Farm Street church, and I shared the joy that others have had of seeing the handsome formal appearance dissolve into boyish grins and infectious laughter. His humour and his spontaneous giving nature are two more reasons why everyone who meets him is prepared to follow him devotedly.

Malcolm Williamson, 1979

1

CHILDHOOD
AND EARLY TRAINING

There are few musicians – and perhaps only half a dozen organists – whose advertised appearance will guarantee a full house in almost any of the world's leading concert halls. One such is George Thalben-Ball, a virtuoso whose reputation has done much to raise the standing both of the organ as a serious concert instrument and of the British musician abroad. Sir Jack Westrup commented in the *Daily Telegraph* in 1935: 'When we have Englishmen who can play as well as this, there is no need to engage foreigners.'

Dr Thalben-Ball has remained a force through many changes in musical attitudes and fashion. He is a link with figures from the distant past; he was taught by pupils of Liszt, von Bülow and Clara Schumann, and by the leading British musicians at the beginning of this century: Sir Charles Stanford, Sir Hubert Parry, G. D. Cunningham, Sir Walter Parratt and Sir Walford Davies. He has numbered among his friends the composers Gustav Holst and Herbert Howells, great organists such as Marcel Dupré in France and Virgil Fox in the United States, and now legendary musical celebrities of the calibre of Sir Henry Wood and Sir Hugh Allen. He has himself taught several of today's leading executants; and he continues to première music composed during the 1970s, just as he pioneered new compositions in the 1920s.

His radio broadcasts, his gramophone recordings and his public concerts have made George Thalben-Ball a household name and he retains a number of important appointments: organist and curator of the organ at London's Royal Albert Hall (a position he has held since 1934); organist of both the City and the University of Birmingham (since 1949); and organist and director of the choir of the Temple Church, London (since 1923, though he had taken

Organist of the future, George Thomas Ball, pictured in his country of birth,
Australia, before the turn of the century.

over as acting organist in 1919 and was thus, in March 1979, able to celebrate his sixtieth anniversary in the Temple organ loft). The Temple Church indeed continues Sunday by Sunday to attract admirers from many countries: admirers who come to hear Thalben-Ball play the organ and direct his choir, in the same way that their predecessors would flock to hear the previous two organists, E. J. Hopkins (appointed in 1843) and Sir Walford Davies (from 1898). Even earlier, the pilgrim George Frideric Handel had often listened in that same building to its eighteenth-century organist, the blind virtuoso John Stanley.

Nearly twenty years after the age at which most people retire, Dr Thalben-Ball's energy seems quite boundless. In 1978 Lionel Dakers, then President of the Royal College of Organists, remarked on his astounding stamina: 'He commutes across the Atlantic with as little fuss as if he were going on the Circle Line from Temple to South Kensington.'

George Thomas Ball, as he was christened, considered entering the priesthood, and likes to think he might have risen high enough in the church's hierarchy to have become Canon Ball. 'Then', he reflects, smiling, 'I should have been one of the big guns of the Church.'

He was born in Sydney, Australia, in 1896, and it was there that he spent his first three years. But he is not a true Australian: his parents were Cornish, away from England temporarily on business. His mother, the daughter of a miller, had been brought up on a farm called Arrallas, off the main Bodmin–Truro road, and she had in her teens been organist of the thirteenth-century church in the small village of St Mawgan-in-Pydar. She relinquished the post when she married, and channelled her own musical ambitions largely through her children. George's father, too, was an amateur musician who, on the family's return to England, adjudicated brass band competitions and conducted concerts at the Crystal Palace, as well as helping to form bands for the Boys' Brigade.

It is not often that Dr Thalben-Ball talks about his early years, but he does remember isolated incidents from his Australian infancy: the time his father rescued an injured gull, put its broken leg in splints and nursed it back to health; and the day a limping

Chinaman came to the house selling onions, and George, to the horror of his parents, followed the poor man up the garden path, imitating his uneven walk.

Young George almost failed to complete the journey to England: he was apparently kidnapped on the way. At Colombo a boat full of peaches drew alongside the England-bound ship, and when the small golden-haired child went to have a look, the native sailors invited him to join them and help himself to their load. He was missing for two days before he was found by a crew member and restored to his distraught parents.

The family, which soon included a fourth member – Sydney, later to become a principal in the Bank of England – settled in London in Muswell Hill, where for many years they lived in Leaside Avenue, just a few doors from the organist G. D. Cunningham. As children George and his younger brother looked forward to the spectacular firework displays which regularly took place over the lake in the grounds of the nearby Alexandra Palace; and they were taken to one of the performances of Tchaikovsky's *1812* Overture in the Great Hall, with massed brass bands, elaborate cannon and rocket effects and fireworks outside which lit up the building's glass roof. 'Quite an exciting business,' Thalben-Ball recalls. His brother later played cricket for the Alexandra Park team, but George preferred to ride horses in Richmond Park.

The boys occasionally visited their grandparents in Cornwall: their grandfather with his brown, wrinkled, weathered face, who drove his pony and trap across the farm, and would take them into Truro as a treat (George developed a liking for jellied eels on these trips). Then there was the day the old farmer called out: 'Syd, go and bring in that log.' Young Sydney was left, so he now claims, 'wrestling with half a tree-trunk lying there'.

Both boys attended a local private school, Highfield, and it was natural that they should also join the choir of the parish church, St James's, where Cunningham was the organist – the same Cunningham who was organist of the Alexandra Palace and later of Birmingham Town Hall. Sydney succeeded George as the main solo boy in the choir.

But it was with a friend of his own age, Harold Ward, that George sneaked into the church one evening after dark and sat listening to one of Cunningham's pupils, Ernest Stevens, practising

George with his younger brother Sydney and their parents. Mr and Mrs Ball, who were themselves amateur musicians, decided that George should learn the piano and Sydney the 'cello, and that both should become church choristers. Mrs Ball's own organ-playing days had come to an end when she married, but her husband adjudicated brass band competitions, conducted concerts at the Crystal Palace, and helped form bands for the Boys' Brigade.

Both George (pictured) and his brother sang as choristers at St James's, Muswell Hill, where G. D. Cunningham, better known as organist of the Alexandra Palace, was organist and choirmaster. Sydney succeeded George as solo boy.

on the old hand-blown organ – a three-manual instrument by Henry Speechley. After a while the boys crept over to the opposite side of the church, to a small American organ in the Lady Chapel. Stevens began to play Bach's Fugue in D at that moment, and young George, who had heard Cunningham play the piece on numerous occasions both at the Alexandra Palace and at the church, and who had played it on his mother's American organ at home, joined in. Unfortunately this American organ was a quarter of a tone sharp. Stevens stopped playing and looked round but, not seeing the young choristers in the dark, shouted to the organ blower: 'Duff, what's happened? Is the wind all right?' 'Yes, sir,' came the reply. Stevens tried each of the stops in turn, to find out whether it was the tuning that was at fault. But no, the tuning was all right. So he tried the Bach fugue again, and again George joined in. A further exchange between organist and blower; more trying-out of individual stops. Finally another attempt, but this time Stevens stopped after the first phrase and Ball, not expecting that, continued for a full three bars before realising that the other organist was no longer playing. 'Duff, the organ played the last bit by itself. What *is* the matter with the thing?' exclaimed the bewildered student. But Harold's hysterical laughter, which he had managed to stifle until then, gave the game away, and the boys 'got a little bit of a wigging for that from Cunningham'.

George was taught the rudiments of music and basic sight-reading by his father. His first piano lessons were from a local music teacher, a Mr Edwards, but he was soon transferred, at Edwards's suggestion, to Cunningham, who taught him his fundamental technique and prepared him for a scholarship to the Royal College of Music. Cunningham was, in GTB's opinion, 'a good disciplinarian and teacher, and a very fine organist – one of the finest this country has produced. In his day there was no one to touch him.'

From the time George was nine, Cunningham made him practise each day for an hour before breakfast and an hour before bedtime. He introduced him to Bach's 'Forty-Eight' and to the Chopin *Etudes*, and GTB will sit down and play these from memory, if asked. For a local concert he learned a work by Chaminade, which he now describes as 'a beautiful period piece, rather like an exquisite antique'.

George Ball was just fourteen when Cunningham took him to

G. D. Cunningham: neighbour, piano teacher, choirmaster, adviser and
friend. According to Thalben-Ball, he was 'one of the finest organists this
country has produced. In his day there was no one to touch him.' GTB
eventually succeeded him as Birmingham City Organist, and like Cunningham he was proposed for a two-year term as President of the Royal College
of Organists.

George was only fourteen when he entered the Royal College of Music in January 1911 on an Associated Board exhibition. The same year he became assistant organist at Whitefield's Tabernacle.

the Royal College to play the music he had been studying: Beethoven's 'Appassionata' Sonata and the Chopin Impromptu in E flat. The boy was at once awarded an Associated Board exhibition, and he entered the college as a student on 9 January 1911.

His principal study was the piano, for which he had altogether four teachers, beginning with Frits Hartvigson, a Danish pupil of Liszt and official pianist to the Princess of Wales. Hartvigson, however, soon had to retire because of ill-health, and GTB had a few lessons from Herbert Fryer. After that came Franklin Taylor, 'a martinet absolutely', a former pupil of Moscheles, Hauptmann and Richter in Leipzig and of Clara Schumann in Paris. For his first lesson with Taylor, GTB took along Beethoven's Thirty-two Variations in C minor, and was somewhat taken aback when he was stopped after the very first chord. The whole lesson was spent on the first phrase of the piece. Taylor insisted on a far stronger wrist movement, and whisked his pupil's hands from the keyboard whenever he found anything to criticise.

GTB's last piano teacher, Fanny Davies, had also studied with Clara Schumann, for two full years in Frankfurt, and was considered not only a most persuasive disciple of the Schumann school, but probably the greatest female pianist of her day. She loved, as Clara had done, to use a pictorial image to make a musical point: for example, in order to obtain from her pupil the correct balance between the outer melodies and the inner 'filling' in Schumann's Romance in F sharp, she described the piece as a duet between Clara and the composer, her part being the tune in the top of the right hand, and his replies the bass of the left hand. Rather than leave the whole final chord to die away with the pedal depressed, she told GTB to repedal so that the two middle parts would be held by themselves, to represent Robert and Clara in union. Her lessons, incidentally, would start at 9.30 in the morning, and finish when she felt hungry – often not till two in the afternoon.

George Ball had been given another piece of advice by his first teacher, Hartvigson – an unconventional answer to a pianist's nightmare. In Liszt's *Totentanz*, for piano and orchestra, the *glissandi* in sixths and octaves in the final cadenza can easily leave fingers skinless and bleeding: but not if the pianist keeps a wet handkerchief in his right pocket and a dry one in his left pocket. Just before the dreaded cadenza he should quickly wipe the keyboard with the wet handkerchief, so making the surface of the keys more slippery and easier on the fingers. As soon as the cadenza is finished, he pulls from his other pocket the dry handkerchief and mops up the keyboard in time for the coda.

GTB's teachers for harmony and counterpoint were Dr Charles Wood, later to become Cambridge's Professor of Music, and Sir Frederick Bridge, organist of Westminster Abbey. Sir Frederick had published a book for schools entitled *Musical Gestures*, a method by which children should learn the musical symbols through movement and mime: thus they would cup their thumb and index finger to represent a semibreve, or add a third finger as a 'tail' to make a minim. Sir Charles Stanford happened to walk into one of Bridge's lessons, and Bridge asked him whether he had seen the new book. Stanford replied that he had, and that he had enjoyed reading it. 'But there is an omission,' he said. Sir Frederick looked concerned and just a little annoyed, and asked if he might be allowed to know what it was. Stanford put his right hand to his nose, then his left hand in front of it, waggled his fingers at Bridge, and replied: 'consecutive fifths'.

Dr Thalben-Ball cannot remember learning much from Bridge, who would look at an exercise and simply say: 'Very good. Do some more.' A fellow pupil, the conductor and composer Eugene Goossens, would copy examples of counterpoint from Bridge's own textbook on the subject and take them to him each week. Because Bridge found nothing to correct in them, they would remain unmarked and would return on a rota basis every few weeks. Only once was Goossens almost caught out, when Bridge found consecutive fifths, and his pupil was sorely tempted to tell his teacher from which source he had copied that particular example.

Charles Wood's class contained three students, Balham, Ball and Brown, referred to by their teacher (in the same way as Bach, Beethoven and Brahms) as 'the three B's'. One day Ball came to the class with a half-pound bag of cherries, and during the lesson he passed them, two or three at a time, under the table to the other two B's. At the end of the lesson Dr Wood looked at him for a moment, then said: 'And next week *you* can behave yourself'; with which he pulled from his pocket all the cherries which young George had thought were being taken by his fellow pupils. On a more serious level, Dr Ball remembers Wood as being a thorough teacher, 'competent in every way, and really excellent for paperwork'.

GTB had learnt the piano – not the organ – with Cunningham, and at college he took organ as his *second* study. His first teacher was F. A. Sewell, at that time the organist of Christ Church, Chelsea. Thalben-Ball was asked to play a Sunday's services there in Sewell's absence, but was not encouraged by the experience. A copy of the Tallis *Responses* was on the organist's music desk, but the choir struck up with the Barnby setting. The poor organist, not knowing the work, had to leave the choir unaccompanied.

Sewell was 'very dapper, beautifully dressed always', and his great strength lay in the reading at sight of complex orchestral scores and choral music containing unusual clefs: 'a very clever little man'. He was an ideal teacher for anybody about to take the ARCO diploma, as George Ball did in July 1913: he not only passed, but won the Lafontaine prize for the candidate with the highest marks for 'tests at the organ'. At that examination, only thirty-nine of the 230 candidates passed.

Later he had lessons from Sir Walter Parratt, the organist of St George's Chapel, Windsor Castle, and Professor of Music at Oxford, whom he had met on his very first day at the college. Sir Walter's 'music class' had assembled, and he was taking the register. 'Mr Crowe', he called; 'Adsum', came the reply. 'Mr Dove'; 'Adsum'. 'Mr Finch'; 'Adsum'. 'Mr Sparrow'; 'Adsum'. 'Quite an aviary we have here this morning.' A voice from the back of the room: 'Yes, Mr Parratt.' ('I'm going to enjoy this,' George Ball thought to himself.)

As an organ teacher Parratt was practical in his advice, without touching more than briefly on questions of interpretation; and he tended to spend much of each lesson discussing topics quite unconnected with the music his pupils had prepared. His intellectual capacity is summarised in the legend that he could perform all Bach's preludes and fugues from memory, and carry on two games of chess blindfolded at the same time. GTB's first assignment was to learn Rheinberger's Sonata in F minor: 'I found it tough going. At that time it wasn't the finger or pedal technique that worried me. It was the discipline needed in organ playing.' Many of GTB's pupils have heard him quote Schumann on this subject: 'There is no other instrument which inflicts such prompt chastisement on offensive and defective composition or execution.'

GTB's second organ teacher, Sir Walter Parratt, was an influential figure in the British musical world. His official posts included Professor of Organ at the RCM, Professor of Music at Oxford, organist of Saint George's Chapel, Windsor, and Master of the Music to Queen Victoria, King Edward VII and King George V. Among his pupils were John Ireland, Herbert Howells, Sir Sydney Nicholson, Tertius Noble, Boris Ord, Sir Walford Davies, Ralph Vaughan Williams and Harold Darke.

Outside the college, an organist whom Dr Thalben-Ball has called one of the world's most brilliant proved to be an important influence. Edwin Lemare, who had become well known for his Saturday evening recitals at St Margaret's, Westminster, continued to give recitals in England after his appointment as organist at the Carnegie Institute in Pittsburgh. George was nine when, accompanied by his father, he first heard Lemare: on that occasion, however, he came away unimpressed after the organist had opened his programme with Bach's Prelude and Fugue in D and played several wrong notes in the opening pedal scale!

Still, he continued to attend Lemare's recitals, and learned from them an invaluable lesson: the importance of careful programme planning. When Lemare played at St Margaret's, the recital would

The staff of the Royal College of Music in 1910, the year before GTB entered the college as an exhibitioner.
Back row: C. Aveling, D. Price, H. Sharpe, W. E. Whitehouse, A. Rivarde, M. Barton, J. Egerton, Mrs Bindon, T. Wotton, A. Holtenhoff, Sir C. V. Stanford, F. Rossi, Maurice Sons, B. Soutten, F. Reekes, D. Wetton
Middle row: G. Garcia, Mrs Hutchinson, Dr Emily Daymond, Miss F. Heywood, F. Pownall, Sir Hubert Parry, Miss A. Elieson, Mme M. Henson, Mlle Themoin, Mme Oudin
Front row: C. Draper, S. P. Waddington, A. Visetti, Thomas Dunhill, F. J. Read, Franklin Taylor, Sir W. Parratt, E. Arbos, F. A. Sewell.

begin dramatically with the dimming of the lights until just the altar remained illuminated. He often began with an improvisation, starting on the quietest stop at the very top end of the keyboard (or sometimes the bottom), so creating a magical silence and ensuring the audience's absolute attention from the outset. Alternatively, he might begin with loud, crashing chords – perhaps with the Mozart Fantasia. Thalben-Ball calls him 'a *real* organist and an astonishing executant', and considers that Lemare's improvisations 'equalled in brilliance and cleverness the great improvisations of Dupré'.

The St Margaret's organ had been built to play orchestral arrangements. GTB played Wagner transcriptions there himself: 'Full swell and tremulant would give the effect of orchestral violins, with reeds underneath to imitate the orchestral wind.' There was one thing to which he always looked forward when Lemare played. A piston was set to cancel all the pedal stops apart from a thirty-two-foot flue which, when played on bottom C, made the air shiver without any true note being audible. Lemare brought this into action at the end of every piece – not simply in quiet music – so that it came to be the indication that a piece was over. For George Ball, these were moments of sheer wonder.

Soon after he entered the Royal College in 1911, GTB was appointed assistant organist at Whitefield's Tabernacle, a Congregational church in Tottenham Court Road, under the Welsh director of music, J. Waugh Owens. The church boasted a large three-manual Noterman organ, which proved excellent as a weekday practice instrument. On Sunday evenings the church orchestra (an amateur group supplemented by professional brass players) gave a thirty-minute performance before the service, for which well-known singers and instrumentalists would be invited as guest artists. George Ball several times took the solo part in Handel or Mozart organ concertos.

He would travel with the Tabernacle's male-voice choir to neighbouring chapels and halls, where he played solo organ items from the contemporary repertory: pieces like the Concert Overture in E flat by Faulkes, Smart's Postlude in D, the *Miserere* scene from Verdi's *Il Trovatore*, or a piece by Neukomm entitled *A Concert on a Lake interrupted by a Thunderstorm*. Occasionally he would play a composition of his own: his *Chanson Erotique* or his Fugue in G minor. Or a piece for which he was later to become renowned:

GOOD FRIDAY
SACRED CONCERT
AT 7.30 P.M.
WHITEFIELD'S

VOCALISTS
Miss Beatrice Jeffreys
Miss Ethel Sinclair
Mr. Leonard Lovesay
Mr. Robert Anthony

ORGAN RECITALS
MR. G. T. BALL, A.R.C.O.
(Including Good Friday Music from "Parsival," "Ride of the Valkyries."

Admission from 6.30 to 7.20 by side-door on purchase of 6d. Programme

Admission Free at 7.20

Mr G. T. Ball, A.R.C.O., plays Wagner arrangements for organ at a Whitefield's Tabernacle concert.

Wagner's *The Ride of the Valkyries*. If no organ was available, he would play some Liszt on the piano, or Raff's Rigaudon in D which, despite its title, he considers 'a rather good piece'. The choir sang anthems, glees and songs, a couple of favourites being *The March of the Patriots* by A. Adams and the *Soldiers' Chorus* from Gounod's *Faust*.

One of GTB's appearances with this choir marked his début as an organist in the Queen's Hall. The Evangelical Union of South America promoted a 'Great Missionary Demonstration' in January 1913, and 'Mr Geo. T. Ball' played pieces by Dubois and Silas beforehand, and Liszt's Prelude and Fugue on a Theme of B.A.C.H. afterwards. He also accompanied the hymns and listened to supporters of the union appealing for £50,000 'for the effective evangelisation of the Dark Continent'.

George Ball composed a number of organ pieces at this time, as well as an Overture for orchestra of which he was – and, one suspects, still is – quite proud. 'Rather Straussy,' he confides, sitting down at the piano and playing the first few bars. He took this to Sir Hubert Parry, the Director of the Royal College, for his comments, and Parry told him to come along every Tuesday for composition lessons. Since he had no other pupils at that time and he died soon afterwards, GTB can claim to have been his last pupil. However, the lessons only lasted a couple of months: Parry could not spare the time each week, so he recommended his young pupil to Sir Charles Stanford, then Cambridge's Professor of Music, but also a professor at the college and conductor of the first orchestra.

The Irishman Stanford frightened some of his students, but this was not the reason why GTB wrote comparatively little music for his teacher. He simply could not find the time to devote to composition, when already he was committed to a considerable amount of piano and organ practice, as well as to concerts and services outside the college. Furthermore, he had each day to travel the long distance between South Kensington and his home in north London. So, whereas his slightly older contemporary Herbert Howells considered composition the most important part of his studies and would consequently be given an hour's lesson, GTB would often be dismissed after ten minutes. In any case, 'Stanford didn't altogether like me,' he now admits. 'I was a little rude to him, I think.'

Putting the memory of Stanford aside, GTB recalls a lighter

moment which he witnessed in the RCM concert hall during an organ lesson being given by Sir Walter Parratt to an organist in his year. The pupil began to play Bach's Toccata in F, with its long opening passage of manual quaver figuration over a held pedal F. But this particular organ student started it with his foot on a pedal E, and continued playing, though it was resulting in extraordinary discords, until the end of the section. Parratt stopped him. 'That was all right, was it?' he asked. 'Yes, Sir Walter,' replied the young man. '*Everything*? It, er, fitted all right?' 'Yes, Sir Walter.' 'You're quite sure?' 'Yes, Sir Walter, I think so.' 'You didn't happen to notice that your foot was on the wrong piece of wood down there?' 'Oh,' exclaimed the surprised pupil, who later became a well-known church organist, 'I never thought to look.'

2

THE MONSTER
OF MUSWELL HILL

Already his teachers could see in George Ball a musician whom they could trust. Cunningham engaged him to play the accompaniment to Brahms's *Requiem* at a performance in St James's, Muswell Hill, and later asked him to play for his wedding. Even more prestigious were Thalben-Ball's first full-length public recitals: two programmes at the Alexandra Palace, which Cunningham entrusted to the eighteen-year-old while he was on holiday in August 1914.

One can see the Alexandra Palace, a large Victorian complex of buildings on a north London hilltop, from the train going north, soon after it leaves King's Cross. J. B. Priestley called it 'the monster of Muswell Hill'. Its extensive grounds have been used for parachute descents, balloon ascents, rifle shooting, massed brass band concerts and firework displays. The Great Hall has housed an indoor cycle track, boxing championships, circuses, a roller-skating rink, pantomimes, flower and dog shows, Sunday school rallies, suffragette meetings and other political demonstrations. Around the turn of the century, bank holiday crowds of more than a hundred thousand would flock to the palace's many attractions.

One of the main drawbacks of the Great Hall, however, was pinpointed in *The Times* in 1878: 'The large central hall of the palace does not in any circumstances recommend itself as a concert room.' In 1905 the *Islington Gazette* complained, following an early performance of Elgar's *Dream of Gerontius*: 'The broad effects of the work, of course, penetrated to the most remote part of the sixpenny seats, but such are the acoustic properties of this vast hall that a thousand and one effects of light and shade were unappreciable half way down from the orchestra.' A further problem was

The Alexandra Palace, where GTB made his début as an organ recitalist in 1914. The regular Sunday afternoon recitals, usually performed by Cunningham, drew audiences of up to three thousand.

noted by the *North Middlesex Chronicle*, which in 1898 thundered: 'The management must put a stop to the cries of the touting boys who infest the place. Serious music is not possible while these youngsters are crying their wares.'

Of course, the resonance, though disturbing in choral and orchestral concerts, suited well the large four-manual Father Willis organ of 1875, which became a popular attraction following G. D. Cunningham's appointment in 1901 as palace organist. Sunday afternoon recitals would frequently draw audiences of three thousand.

Thalben-Ball's début as a recitalist was made with two programmes typical of their period, complete with a number of orchestral arrangements. The recital on 30 August 1914 began with Bach's Fugue in G minor, and continued with Guilmant's *Chant du Matin*, the Faulkes Concert Overture in E flat, d'Evry's *Nocturnette*, the Berlioz *Grand 'Rakoczy' March*, the Fantaisie in E flat by

Saint-Saëns, *Walther's Prize Song* from Wagner's *Die Meistersinger* and, to end, Tchaikovsky's *Coronation March*. War had been declared earlier that month, and it seems strange that the Wagner should have been acceptable in the consequent anti-German atmosphere.

In any case, this was one of the last recitals on that organ. It was not used for the rest of the war, during which time the palace was used as an internment camp, and before it could be played again, the instrument had become the victim of considerable vandalism. Cunningham moved to Birmingham as city organist, and it was not until 1929 that the palace organ was restored and reopened.

Meanwhile the year 1914 saw George Ball an organist and choirmaster for the first time: at Holy Trinity, Castelnau, Barnes, just south of Hammersmith Bridge. Almost at once he arranged a series

Holy Trinity Church, Castelnau, Barnes, where GTB held his first appointment as organist and choirmaster (1914–16). He regularly took the choristers from the church to be used by Walford Davies for demonstration of choir-training techniques at the RCM. One year the boys even joined in the summer camp for the Temple Church choristers in Sussex.

of Saturday afternoon recitals given by himself in aid of the church's 'Choir, Cassocks and Surplices Fund', and another to raise money for the 'Choir Music Fund'. In each programme the centrepiece was provided by another musician – a singer or a violinist – and the recital ended with a virtuosic number for organ. One ventures to wonder, though, how successful can have been Wagner's *The Ride of the Valkyries* when played on the church's relatively small, boxed-in, three-manual Henry Jones organ, even though it had recently been enlarged.

The church choir, drawn from the large Victorian villas which lined Castelnau in the days before the housing estate, which now forms a major part of the parish, was built, consisted initially of half a dozen boys, one bass and a tenor. GTB soon increased its size to a regular twelve trebles, two basses and two tenors, but altos eluded him.

It happened that at college Thalben-Ball was a member of Walford Davies's Saturday morning choir-training class, alongside

The console of the Holy Trinity organ as it is today. GTB spent many hours each week practising at this instrument, and he gave several recitals on it.

such fellow students as Arthur Bliss, Ivor Gurney, Arthur Benjamin, Eugene Goossens, Herbert Howells and Douglas Fox. Howells has described the group as 'a class of the intelligentsia of the college'. Each session would begin with an hour's discourse from Walford Davies on some musical subject. Howells remembers his highly analytical mind: if he were talking about a piece of Bach, he would virtually tell the class what Bach must have eaten for breakfast the morning he composed it. On one occasion he wrote out six chords and announced: 'You will never need any more chords than these six' – a remark which caused some gentle amusement after he had left.

A theory taken more to heart by GTB was based on a picture which, until the war, hung in the Temple Church organ loft. It comprised a range of seven hills, each higher and more distant than the last: the farthest was a mountain peak covered with snow. 'This is how music should be composed,' Walford Davies always maintained. 'It must grow towards each climax, with an ultimate goal corresponding to the snow-capped peak.'

For the choir-training class, he would bring his trebles from the Temple Church, and they would be used as 'guinea pigs'. One of those boys, Albert Fielden Buckley, GTB still considers 'the best solo boy I've ever heard: *I know that my redeemer liveth*, when he sang it, used to be really – *it*'. But, not content with the Temple boys, George Ball asked if he might bring his choristers from Holy Trinity instead. Walford Davies agreed, the Barnes boys were thrilled, and the result was that, while GTB learned from his teacher the theory of training a boys' choir, his own choir was benefiting in practice. After some months the congregation at Holy Trinity was listening to competent performances of Stanford's *Te Deum* in B flat, and Walford Davies was so keen to assist that he arranged for the Barnes choristers to join the three-week summer camp for the Temple choir at Angmering in Sussex, at the expense of the Temple benchers.

At one particular class the anthem was Brahms's *How lovely are Thy dwellings*, and while another student conducted, GTB was delegated to play the organ accompaniment. Knowing that at the Temple Church all large-scale music was transposed down a semi-tone in order to compensate for the high pitch of the organ, he decided to prove that he too could transpose, and he played the organ part in D major. At the end Walford Davies enquired: 'And why, pray, are we not allowed to sing it in the key in which the composer wrote it?' 'I think', answered the young organist, '*you* can best answer that, since that is the key you do it in at the Temple.' 'I was a cheeky lad,' reflects that same organist some sixty years later, 'but I think it bore some fruit, actually.'

The first fruit may have been a concert given in May 1917 by the Pinner Choral Society. Conducted by Harold Darke, it was a performance of Davies's cantata *Everyman* (a work which enjoyed continuous popularity for some years), and the accompaniment was shared at the piano by the composer and George Ball.

Something which impressed Thalben-Ball deeply was Walford Davies's religious dedication, which caused orchestras to laugh at him, but inspired choirs with real devotion. GTB remembers the reverence, almost fear, with which the Temple choristers sang for him. After he had left the RCM and was working with Davies at the Temple, GTB was faced with a soloist, George Piggott, whose voice began to crack alarmingly before the service. He turned to Walford, who went over to the boy and quietly told him: 'You will sing this solo. Jesus Christ will be standing beside you.' The boy processed into church with the choir and, apparently half mesmerised, sang a very fine solo, soaring up to beautifully clear top F's. He never sang another note as a treble.

Walford Davies was admired by the choristers, but sometimes for more worldly attributes. His chiming watch, for instance, given him by the Templars' Union, caused hours of amusement. When he pressed a button, it would chime the time, sounding the number of hours first, then the quarters followed by the remaining number of minutes. Naturally, the boys always asked for a demonstration at 11.59.

GTB learned from Davies not only how to train a choir, but also how to accompany a service. One day he heard the older man playing at the Temple for a performance of a Handel chorus. The organ built up to *fortissimo,* while the choir's efforts were redoubled to match the tremendous volume from upstairs. Suddenly Walford took his hands from the keys, and the choir was left suspended on a thrilling chord. When GTB mentioned this afterwards, Davies advised him: 'Be fearless in the use of full organ when accompanying a choir.'

The Reverend Henry Comber Woodhead: a portrait of GTB's rather alarming vicar at Holy Trinity. In addition to his normal duties, the young organist was expected to play for supper parties in the vicarage.

Holy Trinity was an excellent training-ground for the young organist, but it had its drawbacks. The vicar, Henry Comber Woodhead, used to hold supper parties in the vicarage, for which he expected his organist to play the piano, and this entailed returning home sometimes as late as one o'clock in the morning. In any case the journey from Muswell Hill, which involved a bus ride to Highgate, two trains to Hammersmith and a ten-minute walk from there to the church, was proving too exhausting.

When Harold Darke moved in 1916 to St Michael's, Cornhill, Thalben-Ball succeeded him as organist and choirmaster of St James's, Sussex Gardens, in Paddington. And the new organist found himself in immediate difficulty, for he had expected to be able to continue the ambitious musical performances which Darke had been so successful in directing.

He had been at the church two weeks when the vicar, Prebendary Grose Hodge, informed him that the choir was to perform the Evening Service by Churchill-Sibley. George Ball, fearing what the choir would think of an organist who introduced in his first month

The console of the organ of St James's Church, Sussex Gardens, as it was when GTB succeeded Harold Darke as organist and choirmaster of the church. Note the old-fashioned swell-shutter rods and the lack of modern mechanical aids.

music which was generally considered to be mediocre, tactfully suggested to the vicar that he had heard that the quality of Churchill-Sibley's music was 'uneven', and that in any case money would have to be spent on copies, as the piece was not in the choir library. 'Young man, there is only one captain of this ship, and if I say we are to do Churchill-Sibley, then there is nothing further to be said. Is that clear?' So copies were ordered, and GTB made up his mind that this was to be the finest performance of the work ever to have been given. For six weeks he taught the boys their part. Then came the first full choir rehearsal, at which he had to explain to the men why they were being asked to sing this service. He told them it had been specially requested by a very important member of the congregation, to whom a good performance would mean a great deal; it was therefore up to all of them to make the best of the material. The appeal worked, and while the choir gave an excellent performance, the organist embroidered and elaborated the accompaniment with great enthusiasm and ingenuity. Afterwards the vicar came up and put his arm around him: 'You know, I'm inclined to agree with you; it's not great music, is it? Don't let's ever do it again.'

From that moment organist and vicar had a first-class working relationship and a mutual respect and affection. When in 1919 GTB left for the Temple Church, Grose Hodge said that he felt he must leave too, and became Rural Dean of Central Birmingham and a canon in Birmingham Cathedral.

MUSIC IN WARTIME

War was raging, but George Ball, though old enough to fight, was forced by a weak heart to remain a civilian. He was thus able to continue his studies and his church activities relatively unaffected by world events.

At St James's he was in charge of a large four-manual organ built by Hele of Plymouth, and a good choir of twenty boys and sixteen men. He arranged and conducted performances of Bach's *Christmas Oratorio* and *St Matthew Passion* with Harold Darke playing the organ, and at one performance of the former work the choir included Walford Davies and six men from the Temple Church choir. The two young musicians exchanged places for similar performances of the *St John Passion* at Darke's church.

GTB gave many of the Monday lunchtime recitals at St Michael's, Cornhill, when Darke was away. An all-English programme of November 1918, with music by Parry, S. S. Wesley, Darke, Ireland, Stanford and Wolstenholme, includes a note describing Parry's Fantasia and Fugue in G as 'a great work and one of the most notable additions to English organ music of recent years'. This was actually a rather special piece in George Ball's eyes, since he had played it to the composer at college and Parry had, as a result, altered a number of sections which the young organist had shown him to be unworkable.

GTB also had a hand in Parry's 'Wanderer' Fantasia, which was never completed by the composer. After his death GTB and Walford Davies together rescued and sorted the scattered pages of manuscript and filled in missing bars. Thalben-Ball claims that he composed most of the last page! Now he is more critical of Parry's music: he considers that the organ works rely too heavily on sequential figures. On the other hand, the choral works are 'full of melody and heart and emotion'. He remembers especially well

THE
Parish Church of Paddington
(St. JAMES'S, SUSSEX GARDENS, W.)

BACH'S

CHRISTMAS
ORATORIO

(PARTS I. & II.)

Will be sung by an augmented Choir,

Accompanied by Strings, Drums, and Organ,

On SUNDAY, DECEMBER 16th,
at 5.30 p.m.

CONDUCTOR :—

G. THALBEN BALL,

F.R.C.O. ; A.R.C.M.

MORTON & BURT, Ltd., Printers, Paddington and Willesden.

The new organist continued the tradition of large-scale choral performances with which Darke had been so successful. The 'augmented choir' in this case included Walford Davies and six of the men from the Temple Church choir. The use of 'Thalben' dates from this period, though the name was not confirmed by deed poll until 1924.

ORGAN RECITAL

BY

G. THALBEN BALL, F.R.C.O., A.R.C.M.

ON

MONDAY, NOVEMBER 18th, 1918,

At ONE p.m.

1. Overture   (from the Occasional Oratorio)
   Handel

2. Pastorale   . .   . .   *Cèsar Franck*

3. " I will sing unto the Lord a new song "
   (Judith)   *Hubert Parry*

4. Marche Funèbre et Chant Séraphique
   Guilmant

HYMN

PRAYERS.

COLLECTION FOR THE MUSIC OF THE CHURCH.

5. Chorale Prelude on   " Melcombe "
   Hubert Parry

6. " Rejoice greatly "   (Messiah)   *Handel*

7. Toccata in A flat   . .   . .   *Hesse*

VOCALIST   . .   Miss ETHEL MACLELLAND.

One of the first of many recitals given by GTB at St Michael's, Cornhill, Harold Darke's new church near the Bank of England. The inclusion of a hymn, prayers and items featuring a singer or instrumentalist was then common practice. Incidentally, Thalben-Ball also accompanied the singer Ethel MacLelland whenever she sang to the Treasurer of the Middle Temple, Master Muir Mackenzie, the judge who strongly advocated GTB's appointment to the Temple organ loft (see chapter four).

the beautiful *Lamentations* from *Job* (1892), and would go so far as to say that *An Ode to the Nativity* (1912) is 'a first-class English choral work by any standards'.

On Parry's death in 1918, a few friends composed a 'wreath' of melodies which were woven together and played at the funeral in St Paul's Cathedral. These included an elegy, *Jesu Dulcis Memoriae*, by GTB (not to be confused with his later and better known *Elegy* dedicated to Walford Davies), as well as pieces by Stanford, Bridge, Walford Davies, Darke, Wood and Alcock. The collection was later expanded into *A Little Organ Book*, published in 1924, with royalties being given to the Parry Room library at the RCM.

During his student career, Thalben-Ball made many appearances in college concerts, the first when he was sixteen. On that occasion he played the piano part in Beethoven's Sonata in G minor for cello and piano, with the daughter of the Dean of Norwich, Helen Beeching, taking the cello part. A month later he played his first solo, Liszt's Polonaise in E, and in June 1913 he took the solo part in Bach's Brandenburg Concerto no 5, played of course on the piano, not the harpsichord, in a performance conducted by Sir Charles Stanford. He was heard playing other works by Beethoven, Fauré, Brahms, Schumann, Dvořák, Chopin and Ernest Farrar (a fellow student killed during the First World War). But two performances stand out from the rest, the first being of Liszt's monumental Sonata in B minor, in May 1915.

The second is remembered by Herbert Howells, who always thought that George Ball, when he was a student, looked thin, pale and underfed. One afternoon Howells was sitting at the back of the concert hall under the gallery, listening to an orchestral rehearsal conducted by Stanford. It was a final, pre-concert rehearsal, but Howells had not checked the notice board to see what was to be played. Imagine his surprise, therefore, when his friend, looking quite unconcerned, walked on to the platform. The slight figure seated itself at the piano and proceeded to play from memory Rachmaninov's Piano Concerto no 3 in D minor. Ball had been too modest to mention that he had been chosen to play the work in its first public performance in England by anyone other than the composer. Howells still remembers the loving care with which he coaxed the main D minor melody of the opening pages, while all the time sitting quite still and undemonstratively at the keyboard – just as the composer himself used to perform. The orchestra and the few people dotted around the hall became entranced, and Howells was joined at the back by the Director. At the end Parry jumped up, thumped Howells on the back (his accustomed greeting) and exclaimed: 'God strewth! I hadn't realised we had anyone in college who could do what this boy has just done.' Parry and Stanford were each as impressed as the other, and Stanford told Howells during his lesson the following day: 'That was the most remarkable concerto performance I have heard for several years.' Not surprisingly, the nineteen-year-old pianist was awarded the college's Dannreuther prize of nine guineas for the best performance of a piano concerto.

And this was just one of GTB's many student honours, which included the Challen and Son gold medal and the John Hopkinson gold medal (both for piano and awarded in 1914), the Director's history essay prize (1916), a foundation scholarship (1914), a Clarke scholarship (1915) and Fellowship of the Royal College of Organists (January 1915).

His FRCO pieces, incidentally, give a good idea of the organist's then-standard fare: Bach's Prelude in C (the '9/8'), César Franck's Choral no 3 in A minor (both still cornerstones of the repertory) and an arrangement by W. T. Best of the *Larghetto* from Beethoven's Choral Symphony. The keyboard tests were similar in style to those of today. Only seventeen candidates out of one hundred passed.

Only once did Thalben-Ball appear in public as an organist at the RCM, and that was towards the end of his student days, when in January 1918 he played his own Rhapsody on the Chorale 'Burford', followed by Bach's Prelude and Fugue in G. Indeed, he was still thought of as a virtuoso pianist. Organ items in concerts would be played by Harold Darke, William Harris or Harry Stubbs, all of whom were recognised as church musicians of the future and acted at various times as assistants to Walford Davies at the Temple Church. Then there was Douglas Fox, a star pupil who became organ scholar of Keble College, Oxford, lost an arm in the First World War, then proceeded, as director of music at Clifton College, to train a series of top-class organists. Reginald Foort, later a theatre organist, was at that time playing Reger's Passacaglia in D minor, and other student organists included Arthur Egg (who

THE
ROYAL COLLEGE OF MUSIC
PRINCE CONSORT ROAD, SOUTH KENSINGTON.

PATRON — HIS MAJESTY THE KING.
PRESIDENT—H.R.H. THE PRINCE CHRISTIAN, K.G.
DIRECTOR—SIR C. HUBERT H. PARRY, BART., C.V.O., D.C.L., M.A. MUS.DOC.

COLLEGE CONCERT (No. 584)
(Orchestral)
MONDAY AFTERNOON, DEC. 13th, 1915,

AT 2-30 O'CLOCK.

1.—DANCE-SCHERZO for Orchestra   ...   ...   *Arthur Benjamin.*
(First performance)   (*Scholar*).
(Conducted by the COMPOSER, by permission of his Commanding Officer.)

2.—SONG   ...   The Spectre of the Rose ...   ...   *Berlioz.*
GERTRUDE HIGGS (Berkshire Scholar).

3.—CONCERTO for Pianoforte and Orchestra, No. 3, in D minor, Op. 30
S. Rachmaninow.
1. Allegro ma non tanto.   2. INTERMEZZO, Adagio.
3. FINALE, Alla breve.
GEORGE T. BALL (Clark Scholar).

4.—AIR   ...   On her, my treasure   ...   *Mozart.*
DANIEL JONES (Scholar).

5.—SYMPHONY in E flat, No. 39 (K.543)·   ...   ...   *Mozart.*
1. Adagio, Allegro.   2. Andante con moto.
3. MENUETTO, Allegro.   4. FINALE, Allegro.

CONDUCTOR—
Sir CHARLES V. STANFORD, D.C.L., LL.D., M.A. Mus Doc.

THE EASTER TERM WILL COMMENCE ON MONDAY, 10TH JAN., 1916.

The concert, conducted by Sir Charles Stanford, at which GTB gave the first public performance in England by anyone other than the composer of Rachmaninov's third piano concerto. His performance earned him much praise and the Royal College of Music's Dannreuther prize.

GTB poses in gown and mortar-board after becoming a Fellow of the Royal College of Organists at the age of eighteen.

returned to his native Canada, changed his name to Arthur G. Egerton, and became a respected organist and composer) and Bernhard Ord, the future Boris Ord of King's College, Cambridge.

Dr Thalben-Ball is still thankful that he concentrated on his piano playing while he was at college. In 1950 he told the Royal College of Organists: 'There is no doubt that the finest preparation for an organist is a thorough grounding in piano technique, for most of the problems that confront the pianist apply equally to the organist.'

In perhaps less earnest mood, young Thalben-Ball played the piano for some charitable dramatic productions at Cripplegate Institute: one one-act farce by Robert Meyers bore the title *All on Account of a Lobster*. A couple of years later, in 1916, he took part in several concerts to raise funds for the British Red Cross Society's war effort; one at the Hampstead Conservatoire made a profit of £50 3*s*. 3*d*. Then in March 1918 he played for a combined organ and vocal recital on the large four-manual instrument in St Peter's, Cranley Gardens – the instrument which had for some years been presided over by Arthur Sullivan, and the church in which GTB was soon to be married.

OXFORD UNIVERSITY
MUSICAL CLUB

AND

UNION,

THE MUSIC ROOM, HOLYWELL.

1046TH MEETING,

Tuesday, **NOVEMBER 6th,** *1917, at 8.30 p.m.*

Programme in probable order of Performance.

1. **PIANOFORTE QUARTET** in A minor . . . . . . *H. Howells*

   Allegro moderato, quieto—Lento, molto Tranquillo—Allegro molto, energico.

   Messrs. HERBERT KINZE, FRANK BRIDGE, IVOR JAMES and G. THALBEN BALL.

2. **STRING TRIO** in D major, Op. 8 . . . . *Beethoven*

   Marcia—Menuetto e Trio—Adagio—Scherzo—Adagio—Allegretto alla Polacca—Andante quasi Allegretto—Marcia.

   Messrs. HERBERT KINZE, FRANK BRIDGE and IVOR JAMES.

3. **PIANOFORTE TRIO** in F major, Op. 80 . . . . . . *Schumann*

   Sehr lebhaft—Mit innigem Ausdruck—In mässiger Bewegung—Nicht zu rasch.

   Messrs. HERBERT KINZE, IVOR JAMES and Dr. ERNEST WALKER.

A General Meeting will be held in the course of the evening.

———

The Programme for the 1047th Meeting (Tuesday, November 20th), a Pianoforte Recital by Mr. Claud Biggs will consist of Works of J. S. Bach, Scarlatti, Beethoven, Chopin and Schumann.

Members of the University desiring to join the Club can obtain all information from the Secretary, or from any of the College Secretaries.

C. B. HEBERDEN,

BRASENOSE COLLEGE, *October 25th, 1917.*

PRESIDENT.

SHEPPARD, PRINTER, OXFORD.

GTB has performed with many famous musicians: in this instance as a pianist in a quartet with the composer Frank Bridge.

Parratt thought that GTB ought to try for an organ scholarship, and sent him to Oxford to see Hugh Allen, then organist of New College, though soon to become both Professor of Music at Oxford and Director of the Royal College. GTB was given a cold room in New College, where to keep warm he had to cover the bed with his clothes: and not only with his clothes, for, seeing a curtain behind the door, he took that down and put it on the bed, despite its dusty condition. However, he was woken at 11.30 by Hugh Allen, who came in to ask if he would like to see over the college. 'What the dickens?' he exclaimed, as he peered at the brass rings around the young organist's neck. Anyway, GTB was taken on a midnight tour, and Allen demonstrated the chapel organ.

The next day at evensong, the young man was somewhat shocked by his host's casual attitude to the service. Allen was telling him a story during the first lesson ('about someone who ran away with the cook'), but the lesson finished before the tale had ended. Allen calmly continued the narrative, and only embarked on the *Magnificat* when he had completed the punchline. GTB might have gone to Oxford, but other opportunities occurred in London which seemed more attractive.

The name George Ball, or more often George Thalben-Ball, was becoming more widely known. There had been further appearances at the important concert halls, including two in 1916 at the Queen's Hall with the 'Fight for Right' movement, 'an association of practical patriots' dedicated to 'considering national interests before private preferences'. At one of these, Walford Davies conducted a three-hundred-voice choir.

Solo organ recitals were becoming a regular feature of Thalben-Ball's life, and his repertory increased rapidly. July 1918 saw his first public airing of the Reubke Sonata on the Ninety-fourth Psalm at St Clement Danes – a *tour de force* throughout his career. Then in November he played an all-Bach programme at St Michael's, Cornhill, anticipating a speciality for which both he and Harold Darke were to become especially famed. In fact it was in the following year (1919) that Thalben-Ball played the complete organ works of Bach in a series of recitals at St Anne's, Soho Square: a year, that is, before Marcel Dupré's celebrated complete Bach series at the Paris Conservatoire. George Thalben-Ball was being accepted as a future leader amongst English organists.

4

WALFORD DAVIES
AND THE TEMPLE

One day during morning service at St James's, Paddington, two men came to the organ during the sermon and requested that Thalben-Ball come to the Temple Church to play for that afternoon's evensong at three, since Walford Davies had been taken ill. They said it was 'Cantata Sunday' (the third Sunday of the month, when a large choral work replaced the anthem), and that ten sections of Bach's B minor Mass were to be sung. 'Dr Davies has left a full score on the organ,' they said; 'and by the way, we usually do it down a semitone.' The young organist took the precaution of finding a vocal score which he used for the performance, but, as Walford Davies no doubt realised from the episode in his choir-training class, Thalben-Ball could be relied upon to transpose almost anything at sight, and by all reports he succeeded on this occasion without apparent difficulty.

Walford Davies was described by Percy Scholes as 'a man of whims'. So, although all his energy had for many years been centred on the Temple Church, its music and the welfare of the choristers, he suddenly took it into his head that he was needed, first of all in the newly formed Royal Air Force, which he joined as a major in April 1918 in order, as Director of Music, to organise choirs and bands throughout the Service, and then in his native land, where he became Director of Music for Wales and, in this capacity, chairman in Aberystwyth of a Council of Music representing the various university colleges.

Back at the Temple he had a number of assistants to take choir rehearsals and play for services, the chief of whom was Harold Darke: it was agreed on 23 April 1918 that Darke should receive £200 (half the organist's salary) and a key to the church in return

An imaginary re-creation of the scene at the consecration of the Round Church (part of the Temple Church) by the Patriarch of Jerusalem in the year 1185. This painting by Maud Tindal Atkinson dated from 1912 and hung in the church until 1941, when it was destroyed in the bombing.

for standing by and doing Walford Davies's job whenever he was away. Darke was himself helped on occasions by Harris, Stubbs, Scott Goddard, H. C. Colles and Gerald Bullivant. It would have been natural for Darke or one of these others to have been appointed when it was decided that a more permanent successor to Davies was needed. However, it was Thalben-Ball who was eventually chosen, much to the anger of some musicians who felt that Darke had been shabbily treated. One of them, Sir Charles

Stanford, furiously crossed out the dedication to GTB in his recently completed Fourth Organ Sonata, opus 153, and re-dedicated it to Harold Darke. To understand how such a controversial (but farsighted) appointment could have been made, one must look briefly at the way the Temple Church is administered.

Dedicated in 1185, the church began life as a possession of the Knights Templar, a fighting monastic order founded in 1118 to protect pilgrims travelling to Jerusalem, and responsible directly to the Pope. In 1312 it became the property of a rival order, the Knights Hospitaller, and in 1540, when this order was suppressed, it came under the control of the Crown, by whom the Temple lands were let to two societies of lawyers – the Inner Temple and the Middle Temple. In 1608 King James I granted the freehold to the benchers of these societies, on condition that they maintain the church and its services for ever.

Since then the sovereign, as head of the Church of England, has appointed the Master of the Temple, and the church has remained strictly the private chapel of the monarch and of the two Inns of Court. The Bishop of London has no jurisdiction over the Temple Church, just as the City of London has none over the Temple lands. The Master is in effect chaplain to the lawyers, though he is employed only to carry out certain duties in the church. Responsibility for the fabric and for the running of services lies not with him (however distinguished a clergyman he may be) but with the choir committee, a body set up in 1844 and consisting of the Treasurer and a number of benchers from each society. The organist normally attends meetings, but both he and the Master are invited entirely at the discretion of the committee.

When Walford Davies finally decided to resign in December 1918, the choir committee considered three strong candidates to succeed him: Henry Ley, Harold Darke and W. H. Harris, all in their early thirties. And since Davies had made it clear to Darke earlier that year that he was his chosen successor, the outcome seemed assured.

However, Master Muir Mackenzie, a member of the council of the RCM and Treasurer of the Middle Temple, proposed the name of Ball, whom he had come to know through the college. Actually it was whenever the judge invited a young college soprano named Ethel MacLelland to his house (apparently a not infrequent

The choir stalls and organ in the Temple Church before 1941. This was the instrument heard on the early HMV recordings made in the church. In those days the distance between the two sides of the choir was so great that the *decani* singers would walk across to join *cantoris* in front of the organ for large-scale anthem and oratorio performances.

The console of the old Temple Church organ as rebuilt by Rothwell in 1910. The patent stop-tabs underneath each manual replaced the more normal draw-stops at the sides.

occurrence) that he would ask young GTB to come as her piano accompanist – quite a novel experience for a timid lad, who remembers his mother telling him: 'Don't get involved with any girl.'

GTB received a letter from the choir committee, asking him to put his name forward as a candidate and requesting him to rehearse the choir for a week and play for a Sunday's services. But knowing that Harold Darke had applied, and remembering that the older organist had befriended him in the past (even recommending him as his successor at Paddington), GTB politely declined.

This seemed to impress the benchers, who offered Ball the post outright. But, thinking that Darke must be their second choice, GTB replied that he was unable to accept.

At this point GTB's vicar at Paddington called his young organist aside to tell him that the famous judge, Lord Justice Bankes, had been to see him, to find out what exactly was going on. 'Are you shielding someone?' he asked.

The offer was repeated, but this time with the threat that if Thalben-Ball did not accept, the position would be given not to one of the three other candidates but to an organist from America. The vicar exploded – 'this is stupid' – and the young musician finally said that, if asked again, he would agree to become organist of the Temple Church.

But Lord Justice Bankes had no intention of losing Walford Davies that easily. He strongly supported a compromise which would ensure Dr Davies's continued overall direction, even though he might leave the everyday running of the choir to Ball. In the end the committee devised an arrangement whereby 'Mr George T. Ball ARCM be appointed as Acting Organist under Major Walford Davies', with the £400 salary split, Walford Davies receiving £100 a year and GTB receiving £300. Both Inns accepted this measure in March 1919. And so began four difficult years.

Walford Davies's frequent absences had resulted in a decline in the standard of the choir, largely brought about by the lack of replacements for boys whose voices had broken. George Ball immediately set about putting things right, but the results were compared with those of the choir's peak years immediately preceding the war, and were bound to be initially disappointing. He became discouraged, as Darke had been, by a series of anonymous letters containing such remarks as: 'Your choir isn't a patch on the previous choir . . . You are incompetent . . . The most honourable thing you can do is resign.'

In desperation he showed these to Dr Davies, who blamed himself: 'This is all my fault. I haven't had any time to look after the choir and the boys. It's lapsed, and *I* must take the blame for all this.' Davies approached the choir committee with the proposition that, though the financial arrangement should remain as agreed, he should be allowed to return as 'joint organist' for a while; he and Ball would take it in turns to direct the music, one week each. Then if there were further complaints about standards, they would reflect on him. Thalben-Ball recalls: 'I learnt an awful lot in that time.'

But new difficulties resulted from the fact that he was no longer fully in charge. When he took rehearsals and services one week and Walford Davies took them the next, the choir's loyalties naturally suffered schizophrenic lurches from one choirmaster to the other. In the end Davies would buy the choristers a box of chocolates one week, and Ball would bribe them with a bigger box the following week. Then Walford Davies would sometimes arrive to play the organ for a service, not having attended that week's rehearsals, and Thalben-Ball would be relegated to singing in the choir or sitting in the congregation. The week before a performance of the *St Matthew Passion*, which GTB was to rehearse and direct, Sir Walter Parratt happened to remark: 'I hope you're not putting pauses at the ends of the lines in the chorales. They should just be treated as punctuation, like full stops at the ends of sentences.' 'Yes, we *were* going to,' replied GTB. 'Well, you shouldn't.' So at Friday's full choir rehearsal, GTB told the choir that pauses would not be observed. However, Walford Davies, finding himself with a free weekend, decided to come to London for 'Cantata Sunday' evensong. 'May I play?' he asked his joint organist, who had little option but to agree. In the first chorale he accompanied with pauses, and the choir omitted them – both at *fortissimo* – and thereafter there was disagreement in every chorale. Matters were not improved by the church's acoustic, which made it difficult for either side of the choir to hear the organ.

After the service GTB climbed up to the organ loft to find Dr Davies looking black. But he gave him no chance to speak. 'I think', said GTB, 'that's absolutely unforgivable. I told the choir they were to omit the pauses, and you came in and ruined the performance. I think it's disgraceful.' The older man went down on his knees and prayed, but Ball continued: 'Now, that's not going to atone for what you've done.' Later poor Walford told him he was very sorry.

Then there was the time GTB introduced a new *Te Deum*, Bairstow's setting in D. At the boys' practice, which Walford Davies was taking, the new copies were handed out. When all the boys were ready, Davies said to them: 'Watch me carefully, and do everything that I do'; with which he ripped his copy down the middle and tore it into shreds.

As if there were not enough problems, the Templars' Union, a society of former choirboys who met regularly under the chairmanship of the Temple organist, was split in a bitter argument between some of those who had fought in the war and those who had been, or who sympathised with, conscientious objectors. Thalben-Ball did not become involved, but his own slightly ambiguous position as a non-fighter on medical grounds cannot have made his job easier.

Through the turmoil he persevered. He arranged regular Thursday lunchtime organ recitals, and in January 1920 his *Te Deum* in G was first sung at a Temple service. The monthly cantatas continued, with excerpts from Bach (*St Matthew Passion, Christmas Oratorio* and *Mass in B minor*), Handel (*Messiah* and *Chandos Anthems*) and Mendelssohn (*St Paul, Hymn of Praise* and *Elijah*), followed by the music of Parry, Vaughan Williams, Howells and Walford Davies. For these the whole choir sang from the *cantoris* side of the church, underneath the organ, since the two sides of the choir were then placed much farther apart than they are today.

More and more, the running of the choir was left to GTB. From 1920 it was almost always he, not Walford Davies, who presented the monthly music scheme to the choir committee for approval. Before 1919, in fact, the organist had only been invited into a meeting in order to explain a specific point, and would then leave. Ball, not realising this, walked straight into his first meeting, where one of the benchers offered him a cup of tea. He stayed for the whole meeting, and has attended them ever since.

Discreetly the music lists changed in emphasis. The Hopkins services disappeared, and settings by Charles Wood, Kitson, Ley, Alcock, Gray, Lloyd, Walmisley, Stanford and Parry became the mainstays of the choir's repertory, with occasional appearances of music by Boyce, Kelway, King and Smart. Tudor music continued to be poorly represented, though 'Byrd in E minor', 'Tallis in the Dorian Mode' and 'Gibbons in F' were sometimes sung. To this day GTB refers to music of that period as 'stiff', though he has himself introduced motets by Palestrina.

In Walford Davies's time as organist, Parry regularly visited the Temple with his close friend Dr Emily Daymond. After the composer's death in 1918, Dr Daymond continued to join the congregation whenever Parry's music was sung. Following a performance of *Voces Clamantium*, which GTB had directed from the organ, she complained: 'I was *worried* all the way through – worried about the pitch. Were you transposing it up a semitone?' 'No,' replied GTB, realising that she must be referring to the sharpness of the organ, but waiting to see if she would realise. 'It was *so* sharp,' she repeated and left, frowning. The following year GTB transposed the whole work down a semitone, from G to G flat, and after the service he asked Dr Daymond: 'What about the key? Did it worry you at all?' 'No,' she said warily, 'what's the matter with the key?' 'Oh, I played it down a semitone.' 'It was in G major', she retorted, 'as far as *I* was concerned.'

Dr (as he then was) Walford Davies taking choristers' rehearsal at the Temple Church in 1904. Herbert Howells saw his friend GTB assimilate 'a lot of Walford Davies's brilliance in the organ loft and in choir training'.

Secular concerts were held two or three times a year in the ancient Inner and Middle Temple halls. As early as March 1919, George Ball played the piano with the Templars' Quartet (four former choristers who sang together), and in December 1920 the choir concert was left to him to direct.

But it was not until 1923, four months after the choir committee had discussed a present to celebrate Walford Davies's twenty-fifth anniversary as organist of the Temple, that the final blow was delivered. It was at the choir concert on 10 July that Lord Justice Bankes, who concerned himself closely with the music of the church and was that year's Treasurer of the Inner Temple, stood up before the gathering of benchers, their guests, the choir, Thalben-Ball and the recently knighted Walford Davies, and announced that this would be Sir Walford's last official appearance as organist. Sir Walford looked stunned: apparently he had been given no warning of this decision. But he dutifully wrote his letter of resignation, which was accepted with regret by the choir committee the following day, and by the Inner Temple and the Middle Temple a week later.

A resolution was passed appointing Mr G. T. Ball organist from the following Michaelmas term at the full salary of £400, £200 payable by each Inn; at that time the organists of the Temple Church and Westminster Abbey received the same salary. The new organist's duties were to include directing and practising the choir, instructing the choirboys, playing the organ and conducting the musical service on Sunday morning and afternoon during law terms and on special occasions, preparing the monthly music scheme, attending meetings of the choir committee if required, and taking charge of the organ and the music books.

The choristers had begun to produce their own magazine, *The Knight Templar*, in 1922, and this mentions a great improvement in the boys' tone around the time of the final appointment. The following year the magazine of the Templars' Union, *The Templar*, reported that Mr Ball was 'ably maintaining the traditions of the choir's singing. The boys all love him and work hard for him.'

Herbert Howells saw these years in perspective. Thalben-Ball had 'assimilated a lot of Walford Davies's brilliance in the organ loft and in choir training', and his first task as sole organist of the Temple was 'building up the choir to Walford Davies's heyday'.

5

MASTER LOUGH

Walford Davies had attempted, in 1922 and 1924, to record the choir singing psalms at the HMV factory at Hayes, but the mechanical techniques used at that time produced unsatisfactory results, and the experiment was temporarily abandoned. However, by 1926 electrical recording had been introduced, and the choir committee decided, after some hesitation, to commission a recording by HMV in the church. The benchers, especially Lord Justice Bankes, were very partial to Mendelssohn's *Hear my prayer*, so this was the piece selected for performance. There were three excellent boy soloists who could have tackled the solo *O, for the wings of a dove* – Ronald Mallett, Douglas Horton and Ernest Lough – and it was the last who was chosen by Thalben-Ball.

HMV wanted to sell the record on the top-price 'red label', but GTB persuaded the company that it should appear on the cheaper 'plum label'. Its success over a period of more than half a century has been phenomenal, and both the organist and the soloist now proudly display in their homes the gold discs presented to them in 1962 for their part in the only church choir record then to have sold a million copies.

GTB still compliments Ernest Lough for his great control and reliability under the strain of having to sing over and over again, at a time when editing was not possible and every 'take' had to be a complete performance. And he is not talking about just one session. Six months after the record was issued it had to be remade, since the wax on the master copy had worn out. 'I always thought the first one was better,' admits Thalben-Ball. 'It had a slightly brighter tone. The second is rather slower and the tone of Lough's voice is slightly thinner.' He claims that Lough's voice on the modern transcriptions has lost much of its original quality: 'They've taken away the scratch, and with it the upper frequencies. The voice is softer than it used to be, and hasn't got that cello sound it used to have. It's more flutey now – not nearly so good.'

The record's popularity was brought about partly by its low price, but largely by the superb quality of the singing. Still, sales were certainly not hindered by the story, encouraged by the press, that young Lough had actually died when he came to the words 'and remain there for ever at rest'. Lough was playing football outside the church one day when two elderly ladies asked him where they should go to pay their last respects to 'the boy', together with a subscription towards the Lough Memorial Fund. On another occasion a policeman on duty outside the Law Courts suggested to Lough that, instead of just standing around, he should go over to the Temple and see the spot where that young boy 'was took off like' when he sang *O, for the wings of a dove*. A letter from Switzerland asked whether it were true that Master Ernest had died of consumption at the age of seven, but most of the telephone calls and telegrams received by the Lough household were messages of sympathy.

The other side of the coin was that, years after Lough had grown up, piles of comics would arrive at the Temple addressed to 'Master Ernest Lough'. As a bass in the choir, he would pass on toys and boxes of chocolates to the current choristers (who have included two of his sons).

The record prompted such large congregations at Temple services that the benchers had to introduce a system of admission to the public by ticket only. It was not until 1929 that numbers settled down again.

To modern ears the rich quality of Lough's voice is unfamiliar, and of course it was considered exceptional at the time; nevertheless it represented the best of a sound which was then accepted as normal. The second version of *Hear my prayer*, the one most of us have heard, was recorded when Lough was sixteen, at a period when it was not uncommon for a boy to sing treble until he was seventeen. This produced choristers far more experienced and musically mature than their modern counterparts, and a whole choir of extremely competent soloists. Fifty years later GTB complains: 'It's very difficult now, when voices break at twelve or thirteen, to get a *standard*, particularly a solo standard, from boys who are virtually still babies – big babies, though. They grow so fast.'

Ernest Lough: a portrait of the boy popularly thought to have died while singing at a recording session under Thalben-Ball's direction. Courtesy EMI Ltd.

It would certainly seem that the 'Lough sound' was then produced by many boys in the fifteen–seventeen age-group; similar tone quality can be heard on other early Temple choir recordings, of which *Hear ye, Israel* became almost as popular as *Hear my prayer.* At the second recording of the latter, there was an hour to spare, and the producer asked: 'Could Ernest sing something else?' 'Well,' said GTB, 'give me a quarter of an hour,' and he took Lough into the practice room, where together they prepared the other solo, from Mendelssohn's *Elijah.* Within twenty minutes it was on record.

Thalben-Ball can be heard on these records playing the organ accompaniments, and on others (Schubert's *Hark, hark! the lark* and *Who is Sylvia?* for instance) playing the piano. His real triumph, though, had been in the training of the choir and soloists, for these performances and for the series of recordings which followed, to a level still admired by church musicians the world over.

6

TEACHER AND FATHER

Although not yet a full professor, GTB taught the piano, organ and paperwork at the Royal College from the time he ceased to be a student. Among his piano pupils in the 1920s – some of whom had returned from the war to complete their studies and were actually older than their teacher – were Keith Falkner (later Director of the college), the composer Gordon Jacob, and Sydney Watson (later organist of Christ Church, Oxford).

Jacob's piano lessons were his 'third study', composition and conducting being his chief interests. Dr Jacob claims that GTB had 'already acquired the urbanity of appearance and manner which has been a distinctive and admirable feature throughout his life'. Jacob wrestled with Tansig's piano version of the Bach Toccata and Fugue in D minor; and on one occasion, not having practised enough the week before, he took to his lesson a four-hand arrangement of an orchestral piece, *Bolshevite Dance*, which he had written, 'and the rafters rang with what were then rather weird sounds'. At other times GTB would show his pupil 'prestidigital tricks on the keyboard' which, Jacob declares, 'cannot have failed to show results in some of my more ambitious writings in which the piano is used'.

'A smart young man, coming to college always in morning coat and striped trousers': that is how Dr Sydney Watson remembers GTB from his year of piano lessons at the college before he left to become organ scholar of Keble College, Oxford. Watson studied the *Etudes* of Rubinstein ('they were shockers to play'), and GTB coached him in the piano part of the Fauré G minor Quartet in preparation for a college chamber concert. 'One thing I still remember', says Dr Watson, 'is George's marvellous control of the sustaining pedal. He pedalled the piano with a subtlety that I have seldom heard equalled . . . Very few people now realise what a brilliant pianist George was.' He says it was through seeing GTB

The young professor of the Royal College of Music. GTB's piano pupils at this time included Sydney Watson, Gordon Jacob and Keith (later Sir Keith) Falkner.

combine the organ and the piano so successfully that 'to this day
I describe myself as by profession an organist, but by inclination a
pianist'.

Another young professor at the Royal College, Adrian Boult,
witnessed an extraordinary scene in the concert hall during
rehearsals for a dramatic production being mounted by the students.
'There was some question of an air raid, so George went over to the
organ and did an impersonation of one – most effectively.'

One day Hugh Allen and Sir Thomas Beecham were sitting in
the professors' dining room, when in walked GTB. Hugh Allen
beckoned him to join them, and the Director introduced him: 'By
the way, Sir Thomas, this man's name is Ball.' A couple of minutes
later Beecham turned to the young professor and enquired: '*What*
is your name?' 'Ball, Sir Thomas.' 'Why, how *very* singular,' came
the retort.

It was soon after this that George Thomas Ball paid ten shillings
to have his name changed by deed poll to George Thomas Thalben-
Ball, a name which he had in any case been using for certain of his
public appearances for some years. And it was under this name that
his reputation as a recitalist spread. He was chosen to give one of
the opening recitals in 1923 on the new Henry Willis III organ in
Westminster Cathedral, and he accepted several other prestigious
engagements.

Of greater personal significance, though, were three marriages:
those of his friend Herbert Howells, his mentor Sir Walford Davies
and, finally, himself. Howells had been very ill for two years, but
finally in 1920 his doctors allowed him to marry 'a charming girl
in Gloucestershire', as the composer himself put it. Thalben-Ball
offered to play the organ, whereupon Howells immediately went to
see Canon Cheesman, the vicar of the church at Twigworth, near
Gloucester, to tell him that he would like the beautiful little village
organ to be played by a very brilliant young organist from London.
But, said Howells, he wanted the vicar to allow Thalben-Ball to
play whenever he thought it appropriate, whether something else was
going on at that point in the service or not. As a wedding present
Howells was given a page of music by each of seven composers
(including Stanford, Parratt, Vaughan Williams, Holst and Walford
Davies), and during the marriage vows Thalben-Ball, playing very
quietly, laced up these compositions into one continuous piece.

Evelyn Chapman, the New Zealand painter and heiress whom **GTB** married in 1926. She was, he recalls, 'the most beautiful person I've ever seen in my life'. 'An angel walked on earth': thus reads the inscription on her tombstone.

Walford Davies's wedding came as a surprise to everybody. Margaret, a rector's daughter from Wales, was thirty years younger than Sir Walford, but it was announced that they 'both knew', and that settled the matter. They were married in the bride's father's church of Narberth, with Thalben-Ball and Hubert Hunt, organist of Bristol Cathedral and (in GTB's words) 'a dear old man', playing the organ. The local church choir sang the bridegroom's *God be in my head*. Seventeen years later Thalben-Ball and Hunt together played in Bristol Cathedral for Sir Walford's funeral.

In 1926 it was the turn of the young organist himself. On 4 January, in the presence of the Master of the Temple and with music provided by the Temple choir, he married the painter Grace Evelyn Chapman in St Peter's, Cranley Gardens, a large spired Victorian parish church in South Kensington which has since become an Armenian church. He was forced by ecclesiastical law to reside within the parish, and had consequently to stay in a small hotel in Cranley Gardens for a week before the wedding.

Evelyn, at thirty-three three years her husband's senior, and described by him as 'the most beautiful person I've ever seen in my life', was also an Australasian by birth. The daughter of a wealthy New Zealand wheat exporter, Francis Chapman, she was an only child who had always lived at home with her parents, first in New Zealand and later in England. The honeymoon came as something of a shock: in Bournemouth, Newquay and Torquay she spent most of the time in tears, and on the third day decided to return to her parents to recover.

But soon the couple had settled in a flat at 5 Kensington Park Gardens, and their first child, Evelyn Pamela, was born on 3 October 1927. In a sense, GTB has always had two families: his choir family, and his home family, which saw little of him during his busiest times examining, giving recitals, teaching, broadcasting and running the Temple music. Pam followed her mother as a painter, and eventually emigrated to Australia. Their second child, John Michael, born four and a half years after his sister, became a barrister. As a child he always knew that school holidays would bring one task: he would have to pose while his sister painted him.

Both children were sent to fashionable public schools – Roedean and Harrow – and John went on to study at Pembroke College, Cambridge, before being called to the bar of the Middle Temple.

An older Evelyn Thalben-Ball, painted by their daughter Pam.

He had never been a chorister: he attended a number of preparatory schools during the early years of the war, but even if he had gone to the City of London School he could not have sung as a Temple chorister, since the school had been evacuated to Marlborough College and the Temple Church had no boys' choir. But he always loved music, and later sang for a while as a bass in his father's choir. One of his chief out-of-work activities has, for some years, centred around an old Harrovians' Shakespearian drama group which performs a play every year at the school.

7

MELODIES OF CHRISTENDOM

Radio broadcasting was beginning to figure in the life of the Temple choir. Walford Davies would take groups of choristers, and occasionally the whole choir, to the British Broadcasting Company's offices on Savoy Hill, off the Strand. There they were used to illustrate his talks in the series *Music and the Ordinary Listener*, broadcast nationally on Tuesday evenings from 1926 to 1933, and his schools broadcasts of the same period.

Then, in 1933, when Sir Walford was appointed Music Adviser to the BBC's Director of Religion, a new series of programmes was inaugurated under the title *Melodies of Christendom*, and a large audience regularly listened to the broadcasts which followed the evening news on the fourth Sunday of each month. Thalben-Ball would accompany the sixteen BBC Singers in a wide variety of religious music, from hymns, psalms and anthems to excerpts from oratorios. The singers, who were expected by Sir Walford to treat each broadcast as an act of worship and who never knew exactly what they would be asked to do next, simmered rebelliously but did what they were told. However, Thalben-Ball had a reputation for being quite imperturbable, and able not only to accompany anything at all, but to extemporise whatever type of music was needed: an art still enjoyed by Temple congregations, particularly before the anthem, when GTB continues a tradition begun by Hopkins and kept alive by Walford Davies of setting the mood with an improvised organ introduction.

Thalben-Ball also assisted in Sir Walford's weekly broadcasts of choral evensong from the BBC concert hall. Before one such service Davies said: 'At the end, play a beautiful melody.' GTB knew what he wanted: a long, singable, rising and dipping line,

The first-ever radio broadcast to schools was presented in 1924 by Sir Walford Davies, assisted by eight Temple Church choristers, five of whom are pictured here. In the background is an audience of London County Council schoolchildren. The BBC claims that the broadcast came from Savoy Hill, though one of the choristers not in the photograph, Donald Lea, remembers the location as Marconi House in the Strand. The box in the centre of the studio is the microphone, nicknamed 'the mousetrap'

such as that found in Sir Walford's own *Solemn Melody*. The piece he improvised, which resulted in many letters from listeners, and which Davies said was 'exactly right, absolutely perfect', was the well-known *Elegy*, later published, arranged for orchestra and even adapted for military band. Ever modest, Thalben-Ball admits its similarity to *Solemn Melody*: 'It's a crib of the style, but not of the tune, to be perfectly honest.' He dedicated it to Sir Walford, just as Walford dedicated his own organ piece Interlude in C 'to GTB and all the Templars'.

On the other hand, GTB was not always so mild. One day Walford Davies invited him to supper at Broadcasting House, and at the end asked if he would like to come to the studio and watch that evening's broadcast. Just before he went on the air Davies said: 'Now you're here, I've got an idea,' and he turned on the wind of the organ. 'I'll need you at the end of the broadcast.' As a start he demonstrated the use of cadences: 'Beethoven might have written this,' he explained, and proceeded to play a short example on the piano. At that moment he noticed that GTB had a newspaper propped on the organ desk, so he added: 'I'll now ask Mr Ball to play this on the organ.' GTB jumped, thought: 'What key was it in? D,' pressed a piston and played something in D. 'I'm afraid', said Sir Walford, 'Mr Ball isn't attending. I shall play it again.' 'He's not going to get away with this,' thought Thalben-Ball, and when it came to his turn again, he was ready with full great coupled to full swell. Not only did he play the tune correctly, but he improvised a complete four-part fugal exposition based on the subject, all the time ignoring Walford Davies's frantic mouthing and hand-waving. 'Oh no you don't,' decided GTB, 'I'm going to finish this one.' When he had come to the end Sir Walford said meekly to his nationwide audience: 'I didn't know he was going to do that.'

During Sir Walford's five years as organist of St George's Chapel, Windsor, GTB would sometimes join him in the organ loft, where Davies had insisted that Rothwell's build *two* consoles side by side. During psalms Sir Walford and Thalben-Ball would accompany the choir antiphonally. When large choral works were performed to an organ accompaniment the two organists would together provide the orchestral parts, often with one taking the brass and the other the strings. They would also improvise, one taking over when the other lifted his hands from the keys (which each would do at the most awkward place possible).

In a sense Thalben-Ball was always Walford Davies's assistant, because the older man never properly left the Temple. When GTB went to South Africa for three months of examining in 1925, it was Sir Walford who returned to direct the choir for the four Sundays which GTB had to miss. Sir Walford remained President of the Templars' Union until his death in 1941, and borrowed Temple choristers not only for his regular broadcasts, but to illustrate his Gresham lectures in 1930. And at Windsor he was constantly visited by former Temple choristers, to whom he liked to act almost as a spiritual guardian. Sir William McKie tells the story of Sir Walford's arrival one day at the Royal College. As he walked sanctimoniously down the stone steps across the road from the main entrance the director, Sir Hugh Allen, rushed into the registrar's office: 'Quick, get out the prayer books. Here comes the vicar.'

Thalben-Ball considers Walford Davies the greatest choir trainer he has known. But outside the Temple he was 'a first-class amateur. He'd have the best choirs beautifully trained, but would quite happily say to someone: "Come along and sing in the performance, and bring all your friends." And if they sang wrong notes he wouldn't really worry.'

But GTB has never underestimated his own indebtedness to the man who trained him, the man who was discreetly instrumental in his appointment at the Temple, and who acted almost as a grandfather figure to the choir until the last war – a strange position for Thalben-Ball, but one which he accepted without complaint. After all, as Herbert Howells put it: 'Walford was a very remarkable friend of George's.'

8

ABC OF ORGANISTS

'Darke is bald and Ball is dark': so Lord Darling used to say when anybody asked for a description of the two young organists who, despite their competition for the Temple post, remained friendly rivals until Harold Darke's death in 1976. Thalben-Ball played at Darke's memorial service in St Michael's, Cornhill – a reminder of the days when he had played for the annual St Michael's Festival. Then he would accompany the St Michael's Singers in English music by Stanford, Parry, Vaughan Williams and Rootham, as well as in Brahms's *Requiem* and compositions by Darke. The two men invited one another to play for the Bach *Passions*, either at the Temple or in St Michael's, and they gave organ recitals in each other's lunchtime series. And until his death Darke continued occasionally to deputise as Temple organist when GTB was away.

Both men made many radio broadcasts during the 1930s, doing much to increase interest in the organ as a recital instrument. However, it was Thalben-Ball, not Darke, who came to be accepted as the man to ask to give big opening recitals. It was he who, together with Sir Walter Alcock and G. D. Cunningham, played the opening recital on the rebuilt Royal Albert Hall organ in January 1934: a recital which ended with Parry's ode *Blest pair of sirens*, sung by the eight hundred voices of the Royal Choral Society. His contribution consisted of the Mulet Toccata, an Air and Allegro by Festing, Vierne's *Carillon* and Haydn's Air and Variations in A, 'from the Symphony in D'.

He was appointed curator of the organ and organist of the hall in July 1934, and he gave a complete recital in the opening series in March, ending with a piece well suited to such a large romantic instrument, Liszt's Fantasia and Fugue *Ad nos*. He also included in the programme the Schumann Piano Concerto in A minor, in which he played the orchestral parts and Kendall Taylor was the pianist.

The two sides of GTB: at the organ console in London's Royal Albert Hall, where he was appointed organist and curator of the organ in 1934.

And he performed a then-popular piece, *Maestoso (AD 1620)*, 'depicting the hazardous voyage of the Pilgrim Fathers and the faith that was sustained in the enterprise' (according to the composer Edward MacDowell).

Five days earlier, at a joint meeting in the Albert Hall of the London Contemporary Music Centre and the Organ Music Society, he had given the first performance of a piece dedicated to him: Howells's twenty-five-minute, three-movement Sonata no 2, the composer's only published organ sonata (the unpublished Sonata in C minor was his first opus). Although the new work had been begun in 1932, the composer revised it a number of times and only actually presented it to GTB four days before the recital. They met in the Temple Church and together climbed up to the organ loft, where they sat down at the console and, not having seen one another for a while, began to chat. They talked for three-quarters of an hour, during which time GTB slowly turned the pages of the manuscript. 'Let's try it,' he said finally. 'And what he called trying

Herbert Howells, generally considered England's leading post-war composer of music the Church, dedicated his Organ Sonata to GTB. The two men have been friends since their student days at the Royal College.

'The dignified German': description of GTB as he sits at the harpsichord, moustacheless, bewigged and dressed as J. S. Bach.

it', muses Howells, 'was the most electrifying sight-reading I have ever heard. He played it as if he had been practising it for a month.' Howells, indeed, has a special term for it: 'sense-reading, not just sight-reading', and he says that on only one other occasion in his life has he witnessed a similar feat – by the clarinettist 'Jack' Thurston.

In June of the previous year Alcock and Thalben-Ball had appeared together in the opening recital on the new concert hall organ in Broadcasting House. These two, plus Cunningham, came to be known as the ABC of organists, and when Marcel Dupré gave a recital at the Albert Hall, it became the ABCD.

Thalben-Ball's interpretations of the music of Bach came to be renowned, but few people remember how very closely he identified with the composer – even to the extent of dressing in eighteenth-century costume and wig to impersonate him! The occasion was the Oxford Festival of May 1935, and the production was a drama-tised version of the musical duel between J. S. Bach and Marchand – at least, that was the basis. In fact that battle never took place, because Marchand left Dresden hurriedly before it could; but in this version he actually faced Bach when challenged. Edwin Benbow played the part of Marchand and Thalben-Ball appeared as Bach. Both performed several pieces on the harpsichord, 'Bach' including his own Chromatic Fantasia and Fugue in D minor. In a review of the repeat performance, at the RCM Union's annual 'At home', Cyril Rootham contrasted 'the volatile Frenchman and the dignified German'. Bach won.

In actual fact GTB was popular with Frenchmen: so much so that he was the first British organist ever to be invited to France by Les Amis de l'Orgue, the French counterpart of the Organ Music Society. On behalf of Les Amis, Joseph Bonnet asked him to play at St Eustache in Paris in 1936, and soon afterwards Thalben-Ball gave the first recital in living memory by a British organist in the cathedral of Notre-Dame. There he included a performance of Duruflé's Suite, which he had premièred in England during a recital at St Andrew's, Holborn. It is said that Fernando Germani travelled all the way from Rome to hear the Notre-Dame recital.

Thalben-Ball gave a series of six radio talks in 1939, under the title *Listening to the Organ*. For the last programme a piece had been written by Herbert Murrill for two organists: GTB at the BBC concert hall organ, and the theatre organist Sandy Macpherson in St George's Hall (part of the Queen's Hall buildings opposite Broadcasting House). The two organists could hear one another on headphones, and the idea was to compare and contrast the two types of organ: the piece began with each instrument playing separately in its normal style, after which both players pooled their resources and built up to a grand climax. But Sandy Macpherson, although he played the melody composed for him by Murrill, insisted on accompanying it in his own way, much to the composer's annoyance.

At a previous experimental link-up between four organists (GTB, Macpherson, Reginald Dixon and Reginald Foort), Thalben-Ball had been intended as the soloist in a Handel organ concerto, for which the other players would each provide a different section of the orchestral accompaniment. However, that had been abandoned when it became clear that Sandy Macpherson would never be able to play the notes in the right time. There was an added problem, namely that Foort's organ was out of tune with the others.

After a silence of well over a decade the Alexandra Palace organ, its new electric blowing system replacing the old steam plant, was

Henry Willis III's team of organ-builders surface from the depths of the great Alexandra Palace organ during its rebuilding.

officially reopened by Cunningham in December 1929, and the following month Reginald Goss-Custard was appointed palace organist. Cunningham, his predecessor, felt that the old instrument's majesty had been fully restored, and that the blend of full great coupled to full swell was still its finest feature. Dupré pronounced it the finest concert organ in Europe, and the blind virtuoso André Marchal described it as the 'veritable masterpiece of all modern organ craftsmanship'. Thalben-Ball, agreeing with these judgements, recalls: 'The great mixture-work was very brilliant, and opening the box produced a great roar: so often the swell box is the sinner of an organ – uneven or in the wrong position – but not at the Ally Pally.' However, he says the instrument was always short of wind following the rebuild, even though it possessed 'simply enormous main bellows', and the problem remained even after these were replaced with a number of smaller ones. He makes the same criticism of the Royal Albert Hall organ now.

New 'Ally Pally' organist
Reginald Goss-Custard at his
organ console. Marcel Dupré
considered this to be the
finest concert organ in
Europe.

Many of the Ally Pally recitals were arranged by the organ-
builder Henry Willis III, who had contacts throughout Europe. It
was important for continental players unused to British consoles
that mechanical aids such as pistons should function properly, and
according to Felix Aprahamian, for many years secretary of the
Organ Music Society, the instrument was mechanically infallible.
He still remembers a very brilliant recital there by André Marchal.
    Dupré and many of Britain's leading organists recorded on the
rebuilt instrument, and Thalben-Ball's 1931 versions of Wagner's
The Ride of the Valkyries and Wesley's *Holsworthy Church Bells*
are justly famous: these two pieces, incidentally, were also played
by Cunningham in his last recital on the organ.
    But all was not well. The Alexandra Palace was in financial
difficulties, and recital audiences were nowhere near their pre-First
World War size. The palace management complained about the
high costs of the recitals: costs which included the palace organist's

salary, Willis's maintenance bills and the five tons of coal needed to heat the Great Hall for every performance. In 1933 the weekly recitals were reduced to one a month. And only £125 was raised by a badly supported series of Master Recitals in 1937 to raise money to lower the pitch of the organ, despite the fact that Cunningham, Helen Hogan, Percy Whitlock, Thalben-Ball, Marchal and Reginald Foort all donated their services.

The organ was last heard in public in 1939. It was dismantled in 1944 and is unlikely to be rebuilt yet again. Just the front pedal pipes remain in position – a characteristic if sad end for an instrument which was only playable for one-third of its life.

Another organ now destroyed was the instrument in the Queen's Hall, which Thalben-Ball played almost every year during the Henry Wood Promenade Concerts. His favourite contributions, both there and in the later home of the Proms, the Royal Albert Hall, were Handel organ concertos, particularly opus 7, no 3 in B flat (the 'Hallelujah') and opus 7, no 4 in D minor, which were played in Sir Henry Wood's arrangements. One of the highlights was inevitably the cadenza, composed or improvised by the player, which would include virtuosic passagework for both hands and feet. Thalben-Ball had always to remember that he was being compared with another regular Proms visitor, Marcel Dupré, whose cadenzas consisted of complete suites including double fugues. These were often as long as the whole of Handel's last movement, but though they unbalanced the concertos, they were highly effective. 'He had very clever feet,' comments Thalben-Ball, whose own five- or six-minute cadenzas were given quite as much applause.

On Bach nights he would play the Toccata and Fugue in D minor, the Toccata in F or the Prelude and Fugue in A minor, but there would always be encores – sometimes as many as four – such as the organist's own Tune in E in the Style of John Stanley, Widor's Toccata in F, GTB's version of Dussek's *Andante* or his arrangement of Handel's Overture to Ariodante. He composed his Toccata in the French Style one Monday evening and played it from memory on the Saturday, after his friend Osborne Peasgood had suggested he play what GTB considered a somewhat insipid toccata by Flor Peeters as a change from the well-known Widor. Next time they met GTB was very satisfied at Peasgood's first question: 'What *was* that piece you played as an encore?'

London's Queen's Hall, home before the war of Henry Wood's Promenade
Concerts, at which GTB often played colourful arrangements of Handel
organ concertos.

'GO', command the registration letters on one of a series of American cars owned by GTB between the wars. He has always enjoyed driving, and raced at Brooklands on more than one occasion.

Before one performance GTB was amused by a trick which the orchestra played on Sir Henry, who insisted on personally checking the tuning of each instrument in the green room before the concert. The violinists walked into his room in turn to have their instruments checked, but as each player left, he passed the violin he was carrying to the next in line, who then presented it to Sir Henry. The conductor, without knowing it, only heard one violin!

Of course, throughout his very distinguished career as a recitalist, Dr Thalben-Ball has always had a love more important to him than any amount of solo organ playing: a love for his choir. It therefore comes as no surprise that in conversation he will revert to incidents at the Temple rather than prolong reminiscences of his successes as an organ virtuoso. Thus, during a discussion of his Prom appearances, he will without warning stand up and limp across the room. Turning, he will say: 'That's how Draper used to walk.' William Henry Draper was the Master of the Temple from 1920 to 1930, and GTB still chuckles about a procession during which the choir

GTB's mother, aged eighty-three, in Bournemouth. The family likeness is unmistakeable.

was singing the hymn *He who would valiant be.* The Master was at the head of the procession, and as the choir reached the words 'Let him in constancy / Follow the master' every member, from the smallest boy to the most distinguished gentleman, broke into a limp.

Then GTB will sit down again and describe the time he sang bass in a choral society with Gustav Holst on his right and Vaughan Williams on his left. Holst sight-read his part perfectly, but Vaughan Williams never once succeeded in finding his note. GTB had to lean towards Holst and try to ignore the vocal fumblings in his left ear. 'He was a bit of an enigma, Vaughan Williams.'

In 1931 GTB took a party of twelve Temple choristers and two former choristers to Marseilles, as a change from the annual choir camp in Sussex. One small boy, armed with a dictionary and some schoolboy French, asked the waiter for the bill: 'Donnez-moi le bec d'oiseau, s'il vous plaît, garçon.' Rather charmingly, the head chorister wrote a report on the trip in *The Knight Templar* and, in thanking Mr Ball for making it possible, referred to it as 'a ripping and unique holiday'.

But it was not to be 'Mr Ball' much longer. 1935 was the year in which the Archbishop of Canterbury conferred on him one of the highest honours a church musician can receive: the Lambeth doctorate. And unusually, the ceremony took place not in Lambeth Palace but in the Inner Temple Hall, before a company which included the Lord Chancellor of England, several peers and many distinguished lawyers and clergymen. Ruth Holmes described the scene: 'The beautiful interior of the Inner Temple Hall, with its carved oak and soft light, provided a perfect setting for the picturesque group performing the ceremony, as the brilliant scarlet of the robes worn by the Archbishop and the Doctor of Music contrasted nobly with the deep purple of the ecclesiastical attendants and the representatives of the Law. The Archbishop, Dr Lang, after reciting Latin prayers, quoted in English the short passage, which posterity has left unchanged, pronouncing the candidate to be dignified with the degree of Doctor of Music. After an ecclesiastical attendant had placed the hood round the Doctor's shoulders, the Book of Degrees was signed, and the short ritual closed with prayers.'

Afterwards a recital was given in the church by Dr Thalben-Ball and the choir, including his setting of the *Te Deum*, Bach's G major Fantasia and Prelude and Fugue in A minor, and unaccompanied music sung in the Round Church. It was not long before Walford Davies's old title of 'Doctor', the form of address used by virtually everybody connected with the Temple choir, was being applied to his successor.

Actually he was more than a doctor. In 1937 he was made a Bard of Cornwall at Boscawen-Un, and given the title of Ylewyth Mur. Asked what the words meant, he leaned over confidentially: 'Great Musician, or something awful like that. Cornish, y'know.'

1937 was also coronation year. Nine of the gentlemen and twelve boys from the Temple choir formed part of the four-hundred-voice choir in Westminster Abbey at the coronation of King George VI and Queen Elizabeth. The Abbey organist, Ernest Bullock, and Sir Walford Davies, as Master of the King's Musick, were responsible

Dr Thalben-Ball, robed in his Lambeth doctoral regalia. He received the degree in the Inner Temple Hall from the Archbishop of Canterbury, in the presence of the Lord Chancellor, several peers and many distinguished lawyers and clergymen.

for the musical arrangements; although Thalben-Ball had prepared his choristers, he took no active part in the service. However, he did have a chance to speak to Sir Walford, who pointed out what they had both realised: that the 'Temple sound' completely dominated the treble tone, even though it was being produced by just twelve boys.

At the Temple Thalben-Ball and the choir performed a special recital of coronation music for the visitors from the dominions, and coronation anthems were sung in place of the June cantata. And this was a year in which the choir was in particular demand outside the church. It sang at the Guildhall to celebrate the centenary of the City of London School, the school which Temple choristers have attended since 1900. The first service to be broadcast from the church was heard that year, 1937, as was a radio talk by GTB on Christmas carols.

There is a fallacy that choral services in the Church of England are little more than concert performances by the choir and organist. At the Temple such a criticism would be quite without foundation, since the musical contribution to each service is conspicuously just one of several essential elements. It is balanced by a tradition of fine preaching, by beautifully read prayers and lessons, and by a solemn simplicity which perhaps finds its origin in the monastic architecture of the church building.

That is not to say that musicians and music lovers will not be attracted to this form of worship. In John Stanley's years as organist, Handel was a regular attender at the church, and in the 1930s, Dupré sat in the organ loft several times. Gerald Ellison, whose father had appointed Harold Darke to St Michael's, Cornhill, and who himself became Bishop of London in 1973, used, as a Westminster schoolboy, to be a frequent guest in the loft, where he would sit on the end of the organ bench. He asked Thalben-Ball to give a recital at St Mark's, Portsea, when he became the vicar there soon after the war, and he still joins the Temple congregation whenever he is able. Speaking now of GTB he professes his 'respect for his great gifts and gratitude for the enormous service he has given to the music of the church'.

A somewhat irreverent book entitled *What if They do Mind,* by a gossip writer called Percy Colson, caused something of a stir on its publication in 1936. In a chapter headed 'Let's go to church', the author claimed that the singing of the Temple Church 'makes that of all the other London churches "look like thirty cents" ', and he continued: 'In Thalben-Ball it possesses an organist second to none and equalled by very few, and who is, moreover, a genius at choir training.' Colson approved of 'the self-conscious professional air' of the choir – 'even the smallest choristers have it' – and the emotionalism of the singing; 'their singing of the Psalms is a revelation'. But he attacked the use of 'too much Walford Davies, whose sentimental church music is curiously popular with some organists', and thought that more Tudor music should be performed.

In his next book, *Georgian Portraits* (1938), Colson further asserted that Thalben-Ball had made the Temple choir 'the best church choir in England, which is to say, in the world . . . Hear their stately singing of a Bach cantata or Brahms' *Requiem*, without a conductor and with a rhythm and flexibility that I have found in no other choir, and marvel at what can be accomplished by twelve small boys.'

Those small boys, however, did not have for Colson the admiration which he seemed to have for them. He was somewhat disconcerted when a group of them locked him in the church lavatory!

One Sunday Thalben-Ball arrived in the organ loft for a service to find a stranger. 'Good morning. Who said you could come up here?' he asked. 'Ah, as an old chorister I thought I might be allowed to come up.' 'An old chorister? What's your name?' 'Leopold Stokowski,' 'In that case,' said Thalben-Ball, 'you'd better play the service.'

9

SECOND WORLD WAR

On the outbreak of war, services continued at the Temple with a men's choir. The boys, who had been evacuated to Marlborough College, sang whenever they returned to London for school holidays, and were on occasions forced to rehearse in an air-raid shelter in the basement of the Goldsmith Building.

However, on 9 September 1940 a bomb fell on the clock tower of the Inner Temple library, next to the church, and all services were suspended. Other bombs fell nearby in the gardens, in Crown Office Row, Middle Temple Lane, Essex Court, and on the porch of the Inner Temple Hall, while a parachute mine at the east end of the Middle Temple Hall broke windows in the church.

Not to be deterred, the benchers decided that services should be resumed on 22 December, and the full choir sang on the 29th – the only one in London to do so. More windows were blown out of the church, but still services continued throughout January 1941, by which time it was no longer possible to hear a choir of men and boys in central London. After another suspension the full choir was again singing on Easter Day, 12 April: an emotional occasion, as it was the first time it had met since Walford Davies's death the previous month.

It was the last time it met as a choir for fourteen years.

The night of Saturday 10 May was one of the worst of the Blitz. Bombs damaged the Houses of Parliament, Westminster Abbey and the British Museum, and the Temple Church was gutted by an incendiary bomb fire. The organ was entirely destroyed, the Purbeck marble pillars were split by the heat, and the roof of the Round Church caved in; but the thirteenth-century stone vaulting of the Quire remained intact.

The ghost of Father Smith was said to have been heard playing his doomed organ earlier that evening, and well he might! The

The final years of the old Temple Church organ, parts of which dated from 1683. GTB has described the instrument in motoring terms: 'Full organ felt rather like a Bentley sports car going at seventy when it has a top speed of 120: you felt it had that extra surge of power, which in fact wasn't there.'

instrument dated from 1683, when it had won the notorious 'battle of the organs'. Father Smith and his rival organ-builder Renatus Harris had each built an organ and erected it in the church. Smith's was demonstrated by John Blow and Henry Purcell, while Harris's was played by Giovanni Battista Draghi, organist to Charles II's queen, Catherine of Braganza. But no amicable decision could be reached by the benchers of the two constantly warring societies, the Inner Temple and the Middle Temple. There were even unseemly accusations that Harris had slit the bellows of Smith's organ, and that he had stolen the best pipes from his rival's instrument. In the end Lord Chancellor Jeffreys who, despite his nickname of 'the hanging judge', was widely respected for his learning and culture, was asked to make a decision. Though himself a bencher of the Inner Temple, he chose the organ favoured by the Middle Temple.

GTB played for more than twenty years on that instrument, which had by this century been considerably enlarged in various rebuilds. He recalls that, although in size it was similar to its modern replacement, it was essentially far more of a chamber instrument.

The Temple Church after bombing in 1941: 'The damage to the dear old place is quite heart-breaking,' wrote GTB. Derek Wright (pictured), the last chorister to be accepted before the Temple boys' evacuation in 1939, was the first to be taken into the re-established full choir at Westminster Abbey under Dr Osborne Peasgood in 1943.

'Full organ felt rather like a Bentley sports car going at seventy when it has a top speed of 120: you felt it had that extra surge of power, which in fact wasn't there.' Henry Willis III once told GTB that the organ should be moved further out into the church in order to project the tone better, but Thalben-Ball replied: 'No, I think that's its success. It *is* boxed in.'

It had a wide range of quiet stops which Walford Davies loved to use for improvisations, and which GTB also came to cherish. Sir Walford would 'suggest' an idea on a particular registration and the acoustic would do the rest: Thalben-Ball calls it the 'in-and-out effect', as one beautiful sound gives way almost imperceptibly to another. He has always maintained that 'the nearer we approach the edge of silence, the more lovely the sounds become'. The instrument as GTB knew it had last been rebuilt by Rothwell in 1910, with that builder's patent stop-tabs beneath each manual replacing conventional draw-stops. He was looking forward to having it further rebuilt and modernised, and to having a soft thirty-two-foot flue added in the Round Church.

Actually the ghost of Father Smith may not have anticipated the organ's destruction after all. That story was spoiled by a former chorister, Kenneth Cordell, who admitted that before reporting for fire-watch duty that fatal night he had slipped up to the organ loft and played there for a while.

GTB wrote soon afterwards from Wales, where his family was living temporarily: 'The damage to the dear old place is quite heart-breaking. *That* organ can never be replaced, but I hope that something lovely will eventually come in its stead.'

Meanwhile a piano was placed amongst the rubble of the roofless Round Church, and old choristers held short Sunday services throughout the remainder of the war. When he was in London, GTB accompanied, while the men sang and read the lessons and prayers.

Amid the destruction, Thalben-Ball was given one very personal connection with the past when, in August 1941, he was proposed as a Freeman of the City of London – a title dating back at least to the thirteenth century. On 18 September the Court of Common Council made him a citizen within the Corporation of London. Practically, this entitled his children to educational advantages through the City of London School, and his widow would have been able to apply for financial assistance from the Corporation. His name joined those of Nelson, Wellington, Disraeli, Florence Nightingale, Winston Churchill and, alongside them, tradesmen with picturesque and now almost forgotten occupations: broderer, horner, cordwainer, scrivener, wheelwright and armourer-brasier.

10

AT THE BBC

On the death of Walford Davies in 1941, Thalben-Ball was appointed Musical Adviser to the BBC's Religious Broadcasting Department. During the first two years of the war he had occasionally visited the department's temporary studios in Bristol, and his appointment came just a month before its further move to Bedford.

GTB at once took charge of the Daily Service and the BBC Singers. His office was in a converted hotel, rehearsals would be held in church or school halls or in the Bedford Corn Exchange, and the Daily Service was broadcast from the Lady Chapel of St Paul's Church, which had been refurnished to accommodate the BBC Singers and the recording equipment. Most of the services were unaccompanied after Thalben-Ball discovered that, if he played the organ, he at the console in the church had no contact with the singers under his direction in the chapel.

Eric Fenn, the Assistant Director of Religious Broadcasting, worked closely with GTB: 'We were all of us aware of his quick sympathy with the people he was working with. Not all organists – not even all great ones – know how to set choirs and soloists free to do their own work; nor are all able to subordinate their art to the service of a spiritual theme. Dr Ball has these gifts in a remarkable degree . . . he is able to pick up the mood of a preacher and match it exactly with the choral or organ work which is to follow.'

'Many a time during the war,' continued Fenn, 'one or other of us would draw up an evening service which depended for its effective opening on the singing of a sentence of scripture to which there was no tune; and we only had to talk it over with Dr Ball for him to produce, in an astonishingly short time, what appeared to be exactly the right musical phrase to carry the meaning of the words and lead into the short act of worship.'

Relaxing in a rowing boat on the river at Bedford, where the BBC was based for much of the war.

'This is a difficult job,' said GTB, interviewed in 1951, three years before sixty-eight of these introits were published by Novello in two short volumes entitled *Laudate Dominum*. 'The introits must not sound too modern, nor must they be quite ordinary. On the other hand, the housewife must be able to tune in without getting the impression of anything out of the ordinary.' He therefore used various styles: 'This one I wrote rather in the manner of Palestrina . . . a little of Vaughan Williams in this one, perhaps . . . and this, would you say, S. S. Wesley . . . this – well, just myself.' All are basically chordal to enable the words to be clearly audible. They are still sung regularly at the beginning of Sunday morning services at the Temple.

Another member of the BBC's religious staff was John G. Williams, who in 1943 arranged a series of Midweek Services on the subject of meditation, with a practical demonstration at the end of each. In case the programme should under-run, GTB was always prepared to fill in time with organ music. Before each broadcast he asked to be allowed to study the script carefully, to make sure that his closing voluntary would carry the right atmosphere; he would then jot down an outline of what he intended to play. 'I was enormously impressed by this close attention to detail and sensitivity,' volunteered Williams years later. 'I had the impression that everything he did was the outcome of meticulous thought and never left to the inspiration of the moment.'

Preliminary work in compiling *The BBC Hymn Book* began as early as 1937, when Sir Walford Davies was one of the collection's most enthusiastic advocates. On the outbreak of war the work was suspended, and when it was resumed in 1941 GTB was invited to take Sir Walford's place on a committee of clergy and musicians chaired by Sir Hugh Allen. Representatives of several denominations had submitted about five hundred hymns, which had been sent for comment to a number of leading musicians.

The committee, with Dr Walter Stanton as editor-in-chief, included the BBC's Director of Religious Broadcasting, Dr James Welch, his predecessor Dr Iremonger, who had conceived the idea of the hymn book, Dr Thatcher and Cyril Taylor. Sometimes it would meet in Thalben-Ball's office, which contained a piano. Eric

With musical colleagues from the BBC. Neither Sir Adrian Boult nor Dr Thalben-Ball is sure of the identity of the man on the extreme left, though they think he may have been an organist. From second left to right, the others are: Berkeley Mason, who played the organ at many Promenade Concerts before the war; Leslie Woodgate; Sir Adrian Boult; Basil Cameron; GTB.

Fenn, who occupied the office immediately underneath, would hear
a burst of talk followed by the playing of a hymn tune by somebody
who obviously desired its inclusion in the book. 'Then there would
be another burst of talk, feet would cross the floor and someone
else would play the same tune, as obviously "expecting the answer
No"!' He wrote later: 'That the book ever saw the light of day
was due in no small measure to the quiet, persistent but unobtru-
sive work of Dr Ball.' And indeed the book includes thirteen hymn
tunes composed by him.

GTB was more than a mere musician at Bedford. There was the
day he had to read the national news because the newsreader on
duty was prevented by a bomb on the main line between St Pancras
and Bedford from reaching the studio in time. But in any case
Bedford was a pleasant change from London. Thalben-Ball stayed
in 'digs' on the embankment; his family, who had moved temporarily to Brighton, then to Wales, remained in Merioneth until the
end of the war. He often went rowing on the narrow, swan-filled
river, and in spare moments he liked to explore the surrounding
countryside on a dilapidated bicycle. Once he was riding along in
heavy rain, with one hand on the handlebars and the other holding
aloft a shabby umbrella. He was highly delighted when an irreverent
small boy on the kerb called out: 'Oi, Guv'nor, where's yer tight-
rope?' His colleague John Williams sketched the scene during a
subsequent staff meeting.

One of his jobs at the BBC was to write 'buffer music', so called
because it was used to change the mood between, for example, a
comedy programme such as Tommy Handley's *ITMA* and a
religious broadcast immediately following. He composed eighty
pieces in major and minor keys for various combinations of instruments – mainly piano, organ, string quartet, piano and violin, and
piano and cello – in differing styles and ranging in length from
twenty to seventy-five seconds. These were used extensively for some
years.

He was also asked to compose the music to a radio play in
which the characters, who are dead, hear a trumpet call from heaven
(possibly T. S. Eliot's *The Family Reunion*, at the appearance of
the Eumenides, but GTB cannot remember for certain, and the
tapes seem to have been destroyed). No ordinary trumpet call
would suffice: it had to be something quite strange to human ears.

He thought long and finally asked the BBC to set up microphones in St Paul's Cathedral. He then selected the organ's dramatic *trompette militaire* stop, and on that alone played a series of fast-moving dissonances, mostly sevenths. He continued to play, and as the seconds ticked away, echo caught up with counter-echo until the whole dome was swirling with sound. For the broadcast an eight-second excerpt was used, fading in and out at each end. GTB, who was listening, says it made his hair stand on end just to hear it.

Almost as alarming was a letter he received:

Dear Sir,

I have often lisened to you on the wirles. Cud you recomend me a teacher for the ocheriner? It is the onely instrument my son, aged 16 can play as his nails grows in insted of out and thought you might know.

Yours respectfully

Towards the end of the war GTB lived, when he was in London, in the White House, Regent's Park, which at that time was divided into small flats. One night he awoke at 2.45 a.m. and his mind turned slowly to a recital he was due to give 'live' on the BBC's overseas network. 'Gracious!' and he sprang out of bed, 'it's tonight': and indeed, it was scheduled for 3.30. Still in his pyjamas he threw on his overcoat, collected his music and left for the BBC. He arrived with five minutes to spare, having of course had no time to practise. The listeners were never told that the organ recitalist was dressed in his pyjamas: a new slant on Percy Colson's observation that 'Time does not exist for GTB; he has the delightful faculty of being entirely engrossed with the occupation or companion of the moment and forgetting urgent appointments.'

The BBC celebrated the end of the war with a week of special broadcasts. One of the most important, an Evening Service Thanksgiving for Victory from Scotland, Northern Ireland and Wales on Sunday 13 May 1945, was followed by a speech by the Foreign Secretary, the Right Honourable Anthony Eden, MP. It was a service of addresses, readings, prayers and hymns, with representatives from a number of denominations in all three countries. At the end came a specially composed Victory Anthem, *Sursum Corda*, by Thalben-Ball, which was performed by the BBC Choral Society and Orchestra and the BBC Singers under Sir Adrian Boult. Unfor-

The Reverend John G. Williams's impression of GTB riding his dilapidated bicycle. The mark 6/10 was awarded by another colleague in the Religious Broadcasting Department, the Reverend Kenneth Grayston.

tunately GTB's own family missed that part of the broadcast. They listened to the first few minutes, beginning at 7.50, in which some trumpet fanfares, also composed by GTB, were played, but turned off the radio until it was time for the news at nine and Anthony Eden's speech at 9.15.

Actually the commission was a last-minute decision. Originally Vaughan Williams had been asked to write a Victory Anthem to be performed in Westminster Abbey. However, the piece he wrote included a part for speaker, and although special amplification was installed around the Abbey for the rehearsal, the acoustics of the building defeated both musicians and engineers: either the speaker was too prominent, or he was drowned by the choir and orchestra, depending on where the audience sat. In the end the committee overseeing the celebrations admitted defeat. Sir Hugh Allen turned to GTB and said: 'You've got five days to write something.' 'The BBC people were rather stuffy about it,' GTB recalls. 'Of course, I wasn't a composer. Still, a big committee in London listened to Boult's rehearsal of it, and they liked it.'

11

THE TEMPLE PSALTER

The priceless Father Smith organ was not the only victim of the Temple Church incendiary fire. All the choir's music was destroyed, including most of the copies of the new *Temple Psalter*, which had been published in 1940 and was not subsequently reprinted until 1957.

Both in the BBC Daily Service and in Temple services, the singing of psalms has always been a central aspect of the worship, and this particular publication ought to be studied by all Anglican choirmasters. It is based on a tradition at the Temple Church which dates back to the early years of E. J. Hopkins's time as organist (1843–98). A letter in *The Guardian* in 1848 observed: 'Permit me to point out to your readers a church where they may hear Psalm chanting in its utmost perfection. I refer to the Temple Church . . . [the visitor] will hear no slovenly hurrying or clipping of words, but all as it should be. If he lay aside his Prayer-book he will not miss it, for he will hear every word distinctly pronounced, every sentence clearly and reverentially enunciated.' Edward Hopkins was the choirmaster appointed to train the newly established choir of the Temple, and one of his first actions was to point the psalms, using vertical bar-lines and underlining for stress. Fifty years later, in 1893, towards the end of his long tenure, the first *Temple Psalter* was published.

Walford Davies, appointed in 1898, spent much time cultivating natural speech rhythm and careful phrasing in the psalms – then apparently still an approach peculiar to the Temple. He edited Hopkins's psalter, substituting chants and altering the pointing, and published a number of his own chants in a separate collection, *Chants for Certain Psalms.*

Thalben-Ball continued both to lay great emphasis on good psalm-singing and to revise the actual psalter; indeed, special booklets had to be printed for certain sets of psalms, because so many changes had been made on the original copies. He has always believed that psalms sung to Anglican chant should be highly emotional, and that if there is to be no emotion in their performance they should be sung to plainsong. Many generations of choristers have been told: 'Make the congregation sit up, so that even an old bencher will say to himself, "By Jove, I've never realised before that the psalms were so beautiful or so full of meaning."'

It eventually became clear that an updated psalter was needed, and the 1940 *Temple Psalter* (revised slightly in its 1957 form, and available to the public as *The Choral Psalter*) was Thalben-Ball's compilation.

Only twenty-six of the 150 psalms retain the chants used by Hopkins, but perhaps the most important feature of this psalter is its flexibility, particularly in GTB's own chants, which vary in length and shape according to the meaning, the stresses and the emotions of the words. No longer must a single chant necessarily consist of ten chords, four in the first half and six in the second. The number of chords depends on the words, just as does a rise or a dip in the melody. Indeed, when composing his chants, Thalben-Ball mapped out the words pictorially, so that he had in front of him graph-like representations of the required melodic shape.

Thus in Psalm 14 the words 'There is no God' are sung to four chords, rather than the more usual six, so avoiding an inappropriate stress on 'is'. In Psalm 55 a melodic fall in the final quarter, first in the men's parts, then from the trebles and altos, mirrors the words 'fear of death is fallen upon me' (v 4), 'and be at rest' (v 6) and 'bring them into the pit of destruction' (v 24). Even more unusually, the verses of Psalm 146 are grouped in threes, rather than twos, which means that the chant is sung once to each three-verse grouping in the poetry. And the words certainly do divide in this way, verses 1–3 praising God; 4–6 expressing trust in God; 7–9 dealing with His works; and 10, which is set separately, portraying God as King.

Individual treatment of the final verse is a characteristic of many of his settings, as is the separate setting of the *Gloria Patri,* of which there are a number for choir and independent organ, each designed for use with several psalms: in the Temple a set of psalms is only allotted one *Gloria* at the very end, instead of one after each psalm

– an economy introduced by GTB early in his days as organist.

Of course, the psalter can take only some of the credit for the Temple choir's success in psalm singing. Every member of the choir, from the youngest probationer to the most senior gentleman, develops an instinct as to the way they should be sung. And GTB, whose accompaniments are an important element of each performance, provides embellishments, descants and registrational imagery which all stem from his deep attachment to the words which he first sang as a chorister, and which he has been interpreting for three-quarters of a century.

Those words, though, do appear in various versions. *The Broadcast Psalter* of 1948 was an attempt to provide the BBC's Daily Service with an updated version of Coverdale's translation. GTB pointed the new words and chose the chants, of which thirty-six were composed by himself, twenty-one of those having been taken from *The Temple Psalter*. The detailed pointing employs the same symbols as are used in the other psalter: a dot beneath a weak syllable; a half-bar-line before an unimportant word; spaced-out letters to denote lengthening of a syllable; an accent over a stress; a small figure to signal a group of equal-stress syllables; and extra space between words where a slight pause is desirable. The chants, though, are of traditional design.

Eric Fenn realised how much work was needed to complete this project: 'Time after time I would go into GTB's room – then back in London in The Langham – to find him poring over the script to decide on pointing, or playing chants over to see how they would fit the words.'

12

'A CRY OF FEAR': THOUGHTS ON ORGAN PLAYING

As President of the Royal College of Organists from 1948 to 1950, Thalben-Ball presided at the biannual Presentation of Diplomas ceremony. It was he who handed Fellowship, Associateship or choir-training diplomas to several of Britain's most promising young organists, among them Derrick Cantrell, Lionel Dakers, Christopher Dearnley, Michael Fleming, Peter Hurford, Peter Le Huray, David Lumsden, Noel Rawsthorne, Andrew Seivewright, Dennis Townhill and Arthur Wills.

Thalben-Ball's presidential addresses contained many clues to his philosophy as a musician and as an organist. In the first he expounded on the close association between the Church and the organ, and the instrument's consequent segregation since Bach's death from the mainstream of music: 'Its position lies in a backwater of musical activity and development. Its very nature precluded it from becoming involved in the Romantic movement.' Instead it 'burst forth at the end of the nineteenth century in the works of the German composer Max Reger', who 'is even regarded in some quarters as a twentieth-century Bach'. GTB added, however, that 'while many of Reger's smaller organ works are cleverly devised with a true emotional content and sometimes real beauty, the larger works seem to be full of miscalculations, extravagant scoring and harmonies which are often overloaded and even at times turgid'. Karg-Elert's influence, said the man who had done more than any other organist to bring that composer's organ music to the British musical public, 'is probably much greater than is generally admitted, and he must be given full credit for taking advantage of modern pipe-voicing and control, and for breaking away from the traditional mode of registration'.

Most organ music, he continued, is composed by organists for specific occasions (a voluntary or a recital). When written by a leading composer, organ works are often disappointing: for example, Mendelssohn's music for the instrument is 'musically restrained when compared with the symphonies, overtures and other *Konzertstücke*'. There have been exceptions, the most obvious being César Franck and Herbert Howells; the work of the latter 'contains the essence of music – firmness and stability. It is strengthened by its relation to the great art of the past . . . but is not a pastiche.' But alas, 'today the cry is for originality – a cry of fear, perhaps!'

'There can be no bluff in organ music. The texture must be clear and the style definite. Elaborate scoring for the instrument has been tried, but it has never succeeded in covering weak composition.' And this is where the organ scores, 'as a promoter of discipline and integrity in music', for 'clearness of communication is essential for a good understanding, whether it be of words or of music'. However, 'only occasionally is music direct, and still more rarely is it really inspired'.

In the second address GTB followed a previous remark that 'much of modern music may be hot air' with an even more scathing comment: 'The complexity and variety of sonorous substance that music has now acquired often baffles the experts themselves, many of whom are never profound until they are out of their depth.' Organists, he went on, were now 'reverting to music of the baroque era, or . . . experimenting with dissonance, tone-colour and rhythm'. It was, on the other hand, 'obvious that, for many musicians, including organists, a reverence for the past has developed into a cult which is artificial and exaggerated'.

The third lecture analysed the three demands made upon an executant: mechanical, intellectual and emotional. An organist is limited by his instrument's lack of expressive capabilities, which must be overcome through such devices as varied touch, use of the usually unresponsive swell box, and, in certain cases, *rubato*. 'In chord-playing also a sharply played chord followed by a chord of greater length not only produces the effect of an accent but, in fact, causes the second chord to be actually slightly louder than the first by giving the pipes a better wind supply and therefore better speech.'

GTB's guidance on the choice of stops was to remind his audience to be flexible: 'The choice of registration is mainly a matter of taste . . . what sounds delightful in St Ninian's might sound excruciating in St Cuthbert's.'

He attacked the current ignorance surrounding the early stages of the 'classical revival': 'To "play in a baroque way" has become a fashionable phrase without very much meaning and often [with] very little sense'; and he gave three examples of organists using 'baroque' sounds when they had no very clear notion of what 'baroque' sounds were. He challenged the newly fashionable taste for continental organs: 'There seems to be a greater tendency than ever today, particularly in some quarters, to belittle things made or produced in these islands . . . A very distinguished French organist [Dupré] told me that there are no finer instruments in the world than English organs, a feature of which is a rich diapason chorus and the magnificent effect produced by the *crescendo* of a complete full swell.'

However, he commended those players who were 'moving with the times and experimenting with the new and delightful tones that organ-builders in this country are incorporating in their instruments'. And he summarised: 'I feel sure that to go forward is not to depart from the splendid tradition in organ-building and playing which has held such a high place in our national musical life in the past'; we should 'add the results of new experience and experiment to the old'. But in conclusion: 'I would plead that our organs in design and voicing should be before all else *musical* instruments.'

In his final address Dr Thalben-Ball stressed that mechanical improvements had made the modern organ far more expressive than its counterpart of a century ago, and that England boasted a fine tradition of top players. It needed to be said, though, to those who had dissociated themselves from 'our finest traditions', that 'human nature is incurably romantic and will always remain so'.

13

THE
TEMPLE RESTORATION

For thirteen years, from the bombing of the Temple Church in 1941 to its reopening in 1954, former choristers held a short service every Sunday in the Round Church. Thalben-Ball came to these whenever he could, but more often than not it was left to Alfred Capel Dixon, a veteran of the choir, to direct a group of tenors and basses in adaptations of music written for SATB. Ad hoc choirs under his direction also sang concerts in the roofless Inner Temple Hall and the nearby Niblett Hall. Dixon was, according to GTB, 'a beautiful tenor. As a man, he was an absolute saint – and a very good conductor too.'

From 1942 a quarterly Temple Service took place across Fleet Street from the Temple, in St Dunstan-in-the-West, with GTB at the organ. Choristers from Marlborough occasionally sang during their school holidays, but one by one their voices broke, and the continuity so necessary to a boys' choir was severed. The youngest of those Temple choristers evacuated in 1939 in fact became a member of the re-established full choir at Westminster Abbey in 1943. Thereafter, the Abbey's acting organist Osborne Peasgood twice loaned his choristers for Temple concerts in Niblett Hall.

Temporary repairs in 1944 led to the resumption of official monthly services in the Round Church, but the stonework became dangerous, and the benchers were forced to return to St Dunstan's. There GTB would play the organ, or the piano during the rebuilding of the organ in 1946–7. For five years, though (1945–9), he directed a male-voice choir in an annual broadcast of Christmas carols from the Round Church, and two carol records were cut by HMV.

When restoration of the Temple Church was considered, one of Thalben-Ball's chief concerns was the provision of a new organ.

The seventeenth - century 'Father Smith' organ case in the Temple Church, and the post-war case of the modern organ, which was an intentional copy.

Harrison's claimed to have such a full order book that there would be a six-year wait. Walker's estimated five years.

It just happened that GTB had given a recital at Glen Tanar Castle in Scotland, where Lord Glentanar owned a large four-manual Harrison & Harrison organ built in 1927. Soon after the war, Thalben-Ball met him by chance in Cambridge and asked him: 'How's your beautiful organ?' 'I don't know,' Lord Glentanar replied. 'I'm thinking of giving it away; it's deteriorating through lack of use.'

The organ arrived at the Temple, section by section, in 1953, and was erected in a new chamber twice the size of its predecessor. A new case was built, but the pipework remained unaltered, and thus GTB expected it to sound as it had done in Scotland. 'But', he explains, 'it was in a ballroom with thick carpets on the floor, thousands of antlers in the roof, settees and all that sort of thing. It sounded soft there.' In the acoustic of the Temple Church it was far from being too soft. Certain ranks actually had to be revoiced more quietly.

The greatest asset of this organ, GTB believes, is its wonderful blend: almost any stops can be used successfully in combination – even a sixteen-foot *bourdon* with a mixture. It is thus an excellent accompanying instrument. Its boxes, too, give wide dynamic range, and 'the great reeds are *trombas* – a bit more open than normal Harrison *trombas* – a clear noise'. The only disadvantage of the resiting was the high positioning of the console on the church's north wall: before the war the organist had been little higher than the choir's heads, and had thus been able to direct from the console more easily than he can today.

GTB's earliest memories of the organ date from his first visit to Glen Tanar in the 1930s. After the long journey to Scotland and a good evening's meal, he had retired early to his room. Not realising that the wardrobe was carefully fitted with hangers and hooks for all his clothes, he hung his trousers on the nearest hanger and went straight to bed. Next morning a French valet came to lay out his clothes, and not finding them in their proper places, he enquired: 'But vere are ze clothes, M'sieur?' Thalben-Ball replied sleepily: 'On a hanger.' The valet found them, and turned to him again: 'But vere are ze socks, M'sieur?' 'Oh, I don't know – probably in the pants.' 'But vere *are* ze pants, M'sieur?' asked the bewildered valet.

The Temple Church choir after the first post-war full choir service, on 30 October 1955. The Master, Canon Firth, was ill that day, but his head and shoulders were cunningly superimposed on to the photograph. Ernest Lough (third gentleman from left) is still singing with the choir, and his son Robin appears here in the front row (third boy from left). GTB is surrounded by adult singers who were once Temple choristers: they include George Dixon, David Lewer, Douglas Ratcliffe, Richard Stratton, Jack Berry and Alan Polgrean. A portrait of Sir Walford Davies's predecessor, Dr E. J. Hopkins, who directed the choir from 1843 to 1898, hangs on the wall to the right.

'Oh dear, I expect they're in the trousers.' 'Ah, I see now,' said the valet. 'Ze socks in ze pants, ze pants in ze trousaires, and ze trousaires on ze hangaire; all in very good ordaire.' Except for the shoes (GTB's organ shoes), which the valet held up in disbelief: they were full of holes.

The main body of the Temple Church, the Quire, was re-dedicated in March 1954, and for this service the Westminster Abbey choristers sang with the Temple men. Sir William McKie tells how Thalben-Ball went to the Abbey Song School to rehearse the boys, and without much more than a polite greeting, began the practice. Sir William sat there astounded: his boys were producing the famed

'Temple sound', quite different from their normal tone, and GTB had not needed to say a thing.

For the occasion, Thalben-Ball composed an anthem, *Comfort ye, my people.*

Weekly Sunday morning services were not resumed until January 1955, at which point the benchers asked GTB to re-form the boys' choir which had been silent for fourteen years. Voice trials took place at the City of London School, and the first full practice was held on 7 October, the first service with full choir following on 30 October. At first the boys sang fortnightly, but from February 1956 they were on duty every Sunday, and in December the choir was able to perform Bach's *Christmas Oratorio.* It was perhaps a good omen that the youngest of the new choristers was a son of Ernest Lough, who was himself singing bass.

The choir was in excellent shape for the re-dedication of the Round Church in November 1958 by the Archbishop of Canterbury, in the presence of the Queen, Prince Philip, the Queen Mother, the Lord Chancellor, the Lord Chief Justice and a packed church. The music included GTB's new *Te Deum* in B flat, written for the occasion.

The Temple Church to which GTB had to become accustomed in the 1950s was very different from that of the 1920s. For a start, he had grown to love the brightly coloured decorations dating from the restoration of 1842: 'It looked very handsome. It looks like a bathroom now.' Furthermore, the long echo in the Round Church had been much reduced by new, chalky, sound-absorbent facing on the stonework, so reducing the magical effect of unaccompanied choir singing 'in the Round'.

Even the services had a different atmosphere. When Thalben-Ball took over from Walford Davies, the benchers and their ladies sat separately, and the choir committee 'used to be a very formidable thing'. The choirmen arrived at the church for services dressed in top hat and frock coat; the choristers wore heavy white surplices over dark suits. There were two choral services every Sunday, not one, and fewer but older and more experienced choristers – twelve boys and several probationers. Before the war, Hopkins's *Temple Hymn Book* was used, but when most of the copies were destroyed the benchers decided, rather than have a new edition printed, to introduce *Hymns Ancient and Modern (revised).*

A single Sunday service does give the choir more rehearsal time, but the trend of earlier-breaking voices necessitates more basic note-learning and a smaller repertory. Another new phenomenon is that many former choristers go to university and sever their links with London. Previously many had left to work in the City, and had been able to return to the choir as gentlemen. In 1927 GTB told a meeting of the Templars' Union of his ideal of a choir composed of Old Templars, which would be second to none in the world. Although some of the present choirmen have sung with the choir for many years, more and more GTB is relying on non-Templars to sing the lower parts: not necessarily a bad thing, but not a part of his original dream.

14

'BIRMINGHAM
MAKES ME PRACTISE'

A new commitment was undertaken by Thalben-Ball in 1949, when he succeeded his teacher G. D. Cunningham as City Organist of Birmingham. In January of that year, a few months before his appointment, he had arranged and opened a series of guest recitals. But his connections with Birmingham stretch back to the time of Cunningham's own appointment in 1924. On that occasion Sir Hugh Allen, then Director of the Royal College, and the man most frequently consulted about musical appointments of all sorts, invited GTB to his room after lunch: 'I know very little about organists, and particularly recitalists. A City Organist is needed to succeed C. W. Perkins. I have a list of names. I wonder if you would be good enough to have a look.' The fifth from the top was G. D. Cunningham. Thalben-Ball looked up: 'I see Cunningham is down. I need go no further.' He had helped to appoint his predecessor.

One of the main duties of the City Organist is to give a weekly lunchtime recital on the Town Hall organ – a magnificent romantic instrument opened by S. S. Wesley in 1834. He invites occasional visitors, but gives almost forty recitals each year himself. Thalben-Ball, who has aimed to present at every single recital one piece that is completely new to his regular audience, notched up his eight-hundredth lunch-hour recital as City Organist in 1978. 'Birmingham makes me practise,' he admits.

In the early 1950s he presented the complete organ works of Howells and all twenty organ sonatas by Rheinberger during his Wednesday recitals, and he championed the organ music of Wilhelm Middelschulte, a German contemporary of Reger. Other programmes had themes such as 'English music' or 'French music', and one featured compositions by Lemare, Wolstenholme and Hollins,

Birmingham Town Hall, where GTB gives up to forty recitals each year in his capacity as Birmingham City Organist.

all of whom were born in 1865, the last two totally blind; GTB has always considered Hollins a higher-class musician than Wolstenholme, while Lemare was 'a very clever improviser'.

Every Christmas GTB presented a concert in the Town Hall by the Templars' Male Voice Choir, which would include organ solos by himself, piano solos by Norman Greenwood and piano duets played by the two of them. He still gets up before six on a Wednesday, catches the 7.40 train from Euston, practises on the Town Hall organ from 9.30, gives his one-hour recital at 1.15, and is often back in London for an evening appointment.

The City Organist at his console: newly appointed in 1949, and (opposite) 800 Town Hall recitals later in 1978.

An organ very different from the Birmingham instrument is the Harrison & Harrison in the Royal Festival Hall, which has caused perhaps more controversy than any other since the war. After the opening recital in March 1954 by four leading players, Ralph Downes (its designer), Arnold Richardson, Lady Susi Jeans and George Thalben-Ball, *The Times* commented: 'The full organ has a lean and hungry tone, fiery, brilliant and solid it is true, but . . . the sharp acoustics of the hall would seem to require, just as the critics of the specification said, a fuller diapason kind of sonority.' But all the critics agreed that GTB's performance of the Reubke Sonata on the ninety-fourth psalm was stunning. 'Dr Ball appeared to enjoy bullying the organ,' continued *The Times*, 'which his colleagues had approached with a certain cautious deference.'

Actually GTB started in style. Lady Jeans had left the *crescendo* pedal and the full organ piston on at the end of her final piece, Franz Schmidt's Toccata in C. When GTB arrived at the console he noticed the *crescendo* pedal, which he closed, but for some reason ignored the red light signifying full organ. He stood on the pedals to adjust the bench, with a resulting thunderclap. As he threw up his hands in mock horror, the audience applauded heartily. Then very solemnly he climbed off the bench, turned and bowed, to roars of laughter and renewed clapping.

The following year Thalben-Ball was the first recitalist to introduce transcriptions into a Festival Hall programme, though he also included Liszt's Fantasia and Fugue *Ad nos*. 'Never have I heard such a brilliant performance,' raved *Musical Opinion*. 'In fact, I have never heard so much colour from this organ before.' And the same publication printed a reader's letter a year later, which commented on the instrument: 'The only time I heard any pleasant sounds from it was when our Dr Thalben-Ball showed us what could be done with such a contraption; but then, he could wrest a tune from bagpipes.'

In the quarter-century since then, tastes have changed, and that organ is seen by many as an historic instrument which has helped to broaden the tastes of a generation of organists. Through this period GTB has continued to give recitals at the hall in his unique way. He objects to the predominant *nazard* tone on certain of the great ranks (sixteen-foot *pommer* and eight- and four-foot flutes), which he omits entirely from his piston settings, and he tells the story of the day he was practising for a recital before an orchestral rehearsal. A group of instrumentalists gathered round the console and asked him whether he liked the organ. Not immediately prepared to commit himself, he gave them a guarded 'Yes'. 'Do you?' they persisted, 'because *we* think it's awful.' And they explained that they could not understand why organists insisted on playing two tunes at once, one a fourth or a fifth higher than the other, through the use of mutation stops. After all, no other instrument did this. GTB did just once commit himself concerning one particular stop, when he said: 'It sounds like a lot of dustbin lids rattling together.'

Thalben-Ball's playing at the Festival Hall is the same as his playing anywhere else in one respect: wherever he goes he plays for non-organists. The Canadian recitalist Dr Charles Peaker referred to his attitude as 'inspired common sense'. And one of the lessons which he considers a recitalist must learn early on is the importance of stop-changing and colour variation: listening to a piece played through on one registration is like hearing an orchestra perform a movement at one unaltering dynamic. Bach, who loved to try out the stops on a new organ, particularly any thirty-two-foot reed, would be the last composer to want his music to remain the same colour throughout.

GTB's build-ups towards the end of Bach fugues (usually with full swell, followed by big pedal reeds for the final pedal entry, and full organ for the last chord) have led to accusations that he lacks taste and scholarship. But as he says, it's no use trying to imitate baroque sounds on a romantic organ. One cannot expect from large-scale, loud-voiced mutations the silvery effects of an eighteenth-century organ or a 'classically voiced' modern one. His touch and phrasing, too, are very much geared to the slow actions of bulky romantic instruments, and his rhythm in Bach is far less flexible than that of many modern players. He has always insisted that his pupils be able to play a piece with a metronome – even a fantasia – before any freedom at all is allowed. He has occasionally been asked to play baroque organs on the continent, and has adapted his style to the instruments. However, his pupil Margaret Cobb, herself a fine recitalist, summarised his approach when she wrote: 'He does not allow himself to be *bound* by historical or intellectual concepts. It is *musicianship* that matters, always.'

He does, though, have a special understanding of eighteenth-century English organ music, partly as a result of his playing for more than twenty years on the old Temple Church organ. On the question of ornaments he is adamant. He says that Parratt made his students begin an ornament on the note itself, a practice which GTB believes was the English tradition, dating from at least two hundred years earlier. And in the music of his predecessor at the Temple, John Stanley, 'the tune makes this the only logical solution'.

Audiences expect certain things from Thalben-Ball: little things, like the pause before the first piece of a recital while he puts on his glasses and makes himself comfortable at the console; his almost motionless body contrasting with his extremely active hands and feet; the flamboyant lifting of his hands at the end of a piece. Audiences know that if they applaud for long enough, they will be rewarded with up to four encores; after one particular performance at a Prom in the Queen's Hall, when there was no time for encores, he put on his overcoat to take his second bow, added his hat for the third, his umbrella for the fourth and a suitcase for the fifth. He was only stopped by Sir Henry Wood, who marched on to the stage to conduct the next item.

Then there is his pocket-watch, which he won at the age of eleven in a competition in *Titbits*. He had correctly deduced from pictures the names of twelve Underground stations: for example, a large wooden gate was translated as Highgate; an angry-looking monarch as King's Cross. He was told in a letter that he had won a silver pocket-watch which he could have on payment of half a crown for the chain. Although he also owns a gold watch, a wedding present, it is the silver *Titbits* prize which he will look at ruefully after a Festival Hall recital, when the audience is clamouring for more but time has run out.

A characteristic of GTB's playing which is now almost unique is that, at the end of a piece, he will often release the final chord from the top downwards, so that the pedal note lingers as if caught by an echo. In fact he hates abrupt cut-offs on the organ as much as he dislikes them in choral singing, and this may well stem from his work in the Temple Church, where quiet singing, beautifully phrased with no sharp edges, suits the building's delicate acoustic. He asks his choir for a 'warm ending', and complements it at the organ by running his fingers quickly down the pistons on the final chord.

One further aspect of his playing which today strikes many organists as unusual, but highly effective, is GTB's fondness for sixteen-foot tone on the manuals. Often a solo melody will be played at the written pitch on stops of both sixteen- and eight-foot; in his hymn introductions this is particularly common.

15

THE
ROYAL ALBERT HALL

After the war, Thalben-Ball continued to appear regularly at the Proms in the Royal Albert Hall. He played his old favourites at first, but gradually new ideas were introduced. In 1953 Sir Malcolm Sargent conducted the London première of Jongen's Symphonie Concertante for organ and orchestra, composed twenty years earlier, with GTB as soloist. Two years later, however, he was back with Handel's 'Hallelujah' Concerto, and in 1956 with Bach's Toccata and Fugue in D minor.

Though Thalben-Ball must know the Albert Hall organ as well as anybody, he has unpleasant memories of it. One dates from 1946, when he was playing in a concert with the BBC Symphony Orchestra and Choral Society under Sir Adrian Boult. At the rehearsal for the Bach Sinfonia for organ and orchestra (from Cantata no 29, *Wir danken Dir*), Sir Adrian conducted the opening orchestral passage at a tempo too slow for GTB, who entered at his own faster pace. Boult tapped his stick and asked: 'That's your speed, is it? All right, we'll do it like that tonight.' Before the concert he saw GTB and assured him: 'Don't worry, I've remembered your tempo. We'll do it just like that.' Came the performance and, to the horror of the poor organist, Sir Adrian brought in the orchestra at almost double the agreed speed. 'Oh dear, oh dear,' GTB recalls, shaking his head, 'I had to scamper up and down the keyboard at a terrific rate.' Sir Adrian, while not remembering that occasion, declares that he has never heard GTB play anything but impeccably.

At another Albert Hall concert, Thalben-Ball was playing the Bach Prelude and Fugue in A minor, and half an hour before the start he set up the organ so that he would merely have to press some pistons at the performance. He prepared the choir division for the quiet fugal episodes, and the solo tubas (sixteen-, eight- and four-foot) for the final chord. At seven o'clock he went backstage; the concert began at 7.30. His item started with aplomb – he was playing entirely from memory. He completed the prelude, arrived at the fugue, and dropped down to the choir manual, where he found himself playing on the tubas. In that half-hour before the concert someone had reversed all the coupling tabs at the sides of the manuals, and the solo to choir coupler was in action!

More recently he was the organist for a massed bands concert at the hall. He was due to perform a group of organ solos, but as the organisers were short of material they asked him if he would be kind enough to play an extra piece, Widor's Toccata in F. The hall was packed, and as he was about to enter the building for the concert, a man came up to him and asked if he might sit in the one vacant seat remaining – the chair by the organ. Since he was playing from memory and did not need a page-turner, Thalben-Ball said yes, as long as he didn't move or make a sound. When he arrived at the organ the man asked if he might help. GTB thought a moment and said: 'Yes, there is just one thing you can do. When I nod just before the final pedal entry, pull out this stop', and he indicated the thirty-two-foot pedal reed. 'But when I got there', recalls GTB, 'the man went mad, and started pulling the great reeds and tubas out, while I frantically got them back in again on the pistons. And what's more, he never actually touched the thirty-two-foot. I was really angry over that. The concert was being recorded and broadcast.'

But the Royal Albert Hall has been the scene of many triumphs. In 1967 Cathedral Recordings presented a recital series there, in which three programmes each featured two celebrated organists. Jean Langlais was coupled with Alexander Schreiner, Nicolas Kynaston with Fernando Germani, and Flor Peeters with George Thalben-Ball. And what a comparison that last recital made! Peeters did not play his best in the first half, and he received respectful but lukewarm applause. Then on to the stage walked GTB, whose final item, the Reubke Sonata, was greeted with cheering and a standing ovation.

16

'I TOUT I TAW
A PUDDY-TAT'

Thalben-Ball's recital tours have taken him to many parts of the
world, but surprisingly it was not until 1951 that he returned to his
birthplace, Australia. The Australian Broadcasting Commission
invited him and a number of other musicians, including Otto
Klemperer and Sir John Barbirolli, as part of that year's Common-
wealth Jubilee Celebrations. During his four-month stay GTB
played in all but one of the Australian states.

Advertised as 'the world's leading concert organist', he was said
to have drawn the biggest organ recital audiences since the visit
twelve years earlier of Marcel Dupré. And, like Dupré, he played
Handel organ concertos with several orchestras under such con-
ductors as Dr Edgar Bainton, Sir Bernard Heinze, Eugene Goossens,
Joseph Post, Tibor Paul and Murison Bourn. One newspaper critic
in Melbourne, commenting on the Henry Wood edition of the
concertos (the orchestral parts for which GTB had brought with
him), remarked: 'The listener might have had difficulty in seeing
the Handel for the Wood.' However, Thalben-Ball's performances
of these pieces and of recital music were well received.

The Australians observed this visiting celebrity closely. They
noted, for example, that 'Dr Thalben-Ball remains almost motionless at the console', and 'looks more like a bank manager or
brigadier in civvies than a traditional organist'. His dress for recitals
– white tie, tails and red (not white) carnation – was, he told them,
in memory of Sir Henry Wood, who had dressed for concerts in
the same way. Everybody admired his gold cufflinks, which had
originally belonged to Liszt. Liszt had left them to his pupil Frits
Hartvigson, who in turn bequeathed them to the blind organist
Alfred Hollins. Hollins had them inscribed with his own initials (A

'More like a bank manager or brigadier in civvies than a traditional organist':
the verdict from Australia during GTB's 1951 tour.

one side, H the other) and eventually willed them to Thalben-Ball.
There was disappointment that GTB's use of the Sydney Town
Hall organ's sixty-four-foot reed failed to break any windows.
However, the hall's caretaker and chief attendant, who had worked
there for forty-eight years, said that a photographer had once
broken a window when his flash powder exploded, but never an
organist. That organ, a five-manual, 127-stop Hill, which had been
opened by W. T. Best in 1890, was apparently suffering from
suspect tuning when GTB played it, but the organ-tuner assured
his critics that after a week of practising and a concert, it was to
be expected that the organ would be 'just a little bit ragged'. Dr
Thalben-Ball called it a 'grand instrument', though 'a little
antiquated'.

In Adelaide he was less restrained in his judgement. While he was
practising a fast passage, the heavy action caused him to split a

Dr Thalben-Ball points to the tongue of the sixty-four-foot reed pipe in the Sydney Town Hall organ – said to be the biggest organ pipe in the southern hemisphere.

fingernail. When asked for his comments on the instrument he replied: 'Tonally it's fine, and the pipes are excellent. But its action and control are outmoded.' When, twelve years previously, Dupré had been confronted with the organ, he had at once changed his programme.

In Hobart the Lord Mayor remarked that he had had more experience with organs played by a handle than with the type played by Dr Thalben-Ball. 'I', replied the organist, 'seem to spend most of my time with Handel played on an organ.'

A sixteen-year-old girl in Adelaide persuaded GTB to give a second recital just for her, when she told him that her brother was to be married in London 'in an hour's time'. He reopened the console and played her Mendelssohn's *Wedding March*.

The only mistake he made on the tour was to tell the ABC that he was prepared to play requests. The first that arrived read: 'Would you please play *I tout I taw a puddy-tat*.'

One of the press releases sent out to publicise the tour mentioned that Thalben-Ball wore shoes with two-inch heels which 'enable him to obtain a clearer tone from his pedal work'. Be that as it may, he did wear high heels, partly as a result of having seen the recitalist Jeanne Demessieux play with even higher ones.

'She was a very clever girl,' muses GTB, who once heard a recital given by her in Chelsea Old Church. She improvised a forty-five-minute symphony on a number of themes provided by members of the audience, including Benjamin Britten. 'In the *scherzo* there was no common chord from beginning to end, though it all sounded most impressive.' GTB was sitting between Herbert Howells and C. H. Trevor, and Howells turned to him: 'This is *trick* improvising. She can't *think* at this speed.' They decided that, as long as she kept the rhythm and the figuration going, used enough mixture-work and continued to contrast the colours of the different manuals, the improvisation would sound brilliant. After the concert GTB had to take an evening rehearsal of the BBC Singers. They asked him about the improvisation, so he sat down at the organ and imitated it. He found it quite easy, though it sounded complex. 'She was jolly clever, all the same,' he concedes.

GTB took to Australia music by two American composers, Garth Edmundson and R. L. Bedell. Since the war he has consistently performed music by Americans, from Leo Sowerby to Paul Creston,

Robert Crandell, Seth Bingham, R. S. Stoughton and Avenir de Monfred, whose *In Paradisum* of 1947 he describes as 'a cross between Messiaen and Karg-Elert – but not dissonant in a *hard* way'. He thinks that Pietro Yon's *Pastorale*, though reminiscent of Chopin's *Berceuse*, is nevertheless a useful lull between large pieces on a recital programme, and he declares that Sowerby 'wrote some attractive things'. Asked once whether he played so much American music because he felt it to be significant in the organist's repertory, he replied candidly (and perhaps a little facetiously): 'No, it's more because Americans keep sending me copies.' However, he says that, although he knows of 'no really *first*-rate American organ music', he has come to admire several modern American pieces which are outstanding examples of romantic composition.

At the mention of Canada his face brightens; he calls Healey Willan's Introduction, Passacaglia and Fugue 'a very fine work by any standard', though he knows little post-war Canadian music.

Thalben-Ball has visited North America several times, but perhaps the most acclaimed tour was his first, in 1956. He was invited to make his American début at the Lewisohn Stadium, New York, a week after his sixtieth birthday, with a performance of the Handel 'Hallelujah' Concerto, accompanied by the Stadium Symphony Orchestra under William Strickland. He had to play a specially installed two-manual Allen electronic organ. The audience of 4,500 (including 1,200 delegates to the sixtieth National Convention of the American Guild of Organists, which had invited him) had a better chance to hear him the following evening, when he gave a solo recital at the Temple Emanu-El.

Before leaving for the States, GTB had been wondering what to play at this recital when he happened to meet the pianist Kathleen Long, whom he had known as a student at the Royal College (in 1914 she had won the Hopkinson silver medal for piano the same term that GTB won the gold). She had just returned from an American tour of her own, during which she had been criticised for playing music regularly heard on that side of the Atlantic. Her audiences would have preferred a British musician to play British music.

Thalben-Ball took this as a warning and decided to make sure that at least one piece would be heard in the United States for the

GTB discusses a portrait of the artist Datillo Rubbo painted by his wife Evelyn. With him is Anthony Tuckson, assistant to the Director of the New South Wales Art Gallery.

very first time: he composed it specially. And he made his Variations on a Theme by Paganini so difficult that virtually no other organist could play them. Based on Paganini's Caprice in A minor, the work consists of the theme and eight variations, all played on the pedals alone, a ninth variation for pedals and drone (produced by a sustainer stop or, more usually, two pencils wedged into the keys), and a final toccata for hands and feet.

Audiences at both Birmingham Town Hall and the Royal Festival Hall had previews of this phenomenally difficult piece in March, but Thalben-Ball's performance at New York's Temple Emanu-El in June was announced as the 'world première'. The variation requiring the pencils caused some amusement after the recital when the popular American organ virtuoso Virgil Fox, in an after-dinner speech, enquired how it had been possible for Dr Thalben-Ball to play so many notes at once when his hands had been visible all the time, pulling out stops or holding on to the bench. In his reply GTB explained that he had been inspired by Bach's 'Wedge' Fugue – an allusion understood by most of the organists present, since they, unlike Fox, had been in a position to see the console. They all laughed, but not nearly as much as they did when the bewildered American player stood up again and complained that his question had still not been answered.

Nowadays Thalben-Ball only performs the Variations on organs he knows well. The pedal part includes top G's, which are unplayable on F-compass pedal boards: at Peterborough Cathedral GTB had to add notes on the manuals. And on organs with wide individual pedals, he says, it is difficult to play the fast passages cleanly. He always makes sure that he is wearing his organ shoes (the ones with high heels, tapered towards the heel): the passages in thirds in each foot could not be tackled with normal walking shoes.

Alec Wyton, then organist of the Cathedral of St John the Divine, New York, showed Thalben-Ball around the city and told its inhabitants that this Englishman had 'one of the most prodigious pedal techniques in the world'. GTB replied that in earlier years he had loved to dance, and that this had helped his pedal technique. 'You need to be very supple, you know, with your ankles.'

Although the New Yorkers welcomed their English guest with true American warmth, they did overlook one small police sign outside the Lewisohn Stadium, which Thalben-Ball noticed with horror when he arrived. It read: 'No Ball Playing'. He looked at Alec Wyton: 'So I'm not appearing tonight after all?'

The year following the American success he gave a recital in the Temple Church to Americans and Canadians who had come to London for the first International Organ Congress, a large-scale affair administered by committees headed by the organists of Westminster Abbey and St Paul's, with the Queen Mother as Patron.

When American organists visit England GTB will often invite them to give a recital at Birmingham Town Hall – a doubtful privilege, perhaps, since, despite Thalben-Ball's good intentions, both audience and newspaper critics tend to compare the unfortunate visitor with their regular organist. Thus in 1956 J. F. Waterhouse wrote in the *Birmingham Post*: 'Dr Thalben-Ball, whether or not one invariably agrees with his interpretations, is always master-musician as well as virtuoso. Young Mr Fox's virtuosity is phenomenal . . . but his musicianship is still either far from maturity or unduly subservient to his virtuosity.' Exit Virgil Fox.

17

THE MUSICAL
PERFECTIONIST

Organists giving recitals at London's Westminster Cathedral are asked to practise after the building has been closed for the night. They must thus make sure that they leave enough lights on before they start to find their way out again in the middle of the night. The evening before one of his many recitals there, GTB walked along the north gallery from the high altar in the east to the console at the west end, turning on the lights as he went. He arrived safely, did three hours' practice, turned off the blower and console lights, and realised that the cathedral was in total darkness: someone had switched off all the lights at the mains, which meant that he had to feel his way back along the narrow gallery with only the odd eerie candle flickering far below. Reaching the east end, he groped his way down the stone staircase. He stumbled against the door leading into the choir, but whoever had locked up that evening had done a thorough job: he could not get out that way. So he crept on down the remainder of the dusty staircase into the crypt and, he hoped, an alternative exit. He could just see four tiny red lights, and he went towards them. Then he hit something hard, and his eyes focused themselves – on four coffins, which he later learned were awaiting a funeral the next day. 'Gracious, where *am* I?' he thought, trying not to panic and not to knock over the coffins. He turned slowly, made his way up the steps again, along the gallery, through those creaking doors, around that sudden corner with the drop dimly visible, through the iron gate and eventually back to the console. It was 2.30 in the morning before a watchman appeared at the far end of the cathedral with a torch, and Dr Thalben-Ball was able to attract his attention by shouting the length of the great echoing nave. 'A slightly gruesome experience,' he admits.

Right until the death in 1971 of GTB's 'counterpart' in France, Marcel Dupré, the two would send one another Christmas cards. 'Dupré was always very nice to me,' says Thalben-Ball, the younger of the two by nine years. GTB's respect for the Frenchman was greatly enhanced when he walked into St Mark's, North Audley Street, to meet him for dinner. Dupré was practising for a BBC broadcast, and was at that moment improvising a fugue. On their way to dinner Thalben-Ball asked him how much of the fugue he could remember, to which Dupré replied that the exposition was still absolutely clear in his mind. They returned to the organ, and though it was by that time half an hour since he had played it, Dupré reproduced his improvisation precisely. He had 'a very unusual memory'. However, GTB had heard him play years earlier at the Royal College of Music, and then 'he forgot in four of the five pieces he was playing by heart'.

When, recently, Thalben-Ball was one of the judges for the Grand Prix de Chartres, the prestigious international organ competition, he disagreed with the chairman of the adjudicators, Pierre Cochereau, who rang his bell every time a competitor had a memory lapse. GTB pointed out that in a recital at the RCM Marcel Dupré had done the same thing, but had improvised himself right. He 'improvised extremely good César Franck' in the *Pièce Héroïque.*

GTB shows some modesty when he talks of Dupré's phenomenal memory. His pupil Paul Murray tells of the occasion when GTB provided Dupré with a purposely diatonic improvisation theme. 'He played a very nice four-part fugue, and did a reasonably good toccata, but there were none of the brilliant fireworks one usually associates with Dupré, because there were no chromatics or rapid passagework.' The next day Murray discussed this with Thalben-Ball, and 'GTB played a good deal of what Dupré had done the night before'.

GTB has often examined at the Royal College of Music and the Royal College of Organists, as well as for the Associated Board. At one session in a school the first girl came in and promptly fainted. Fortunately he caught her and carried her out into the corridor, where the other candidates were waiting. 'All the other candidates fainted – well, two did, anyway,' he corrects himself with a laugh, 'so I invited them all in, and we had a talk.'

Until recently the examiners at RCO examinations were hidden

Dr Thalben-Ball wrote *Edwardia* in 1974, as his contribution to a collection of eleven pieces for organ entitled *Hovingham Sketches*. A bound copy of the manuscript was presented to Her Royal Highness The Duchess of Kent, who is herself an organist, at the annual dinner of the Royal College of Organists at the Savoy Hotel, London. The title of the piece refers equally to its Elgarian style and to the name of the husband of its dedicatee.

from the candidates by a screen. GTB says he could always tell the female candidates, because they trod on the pedals as they levered themselves on to the stool: he peeped over the screen to confirm the theory.

But on another occasion it was Cunningham who looked over the screen – and for another reason. He and his colleagues heard a candidate enter and the invigilator say: 'Please start when you are ready.' This was followed by: 'Click-ick-ick, Click-ick-ick, Click-ick-ick-ick, Click-ick-ick . . .' Curiosity won and he peered over. He reported back to the other examiners: 'She's playing the opening pedal solo of the Bach Prelude in C minor without any stops out! And we'll have to give her full marks, because I haven't detected a single mistake.'

A former pupil, Peter Goodman, City Organist of Hull, remembers how carefully he was prepared by GTB for his FRCO. Thalben-Ball even chose the registrations. But normally he expected his pupils to work on their own, and to learn a substantial new piece every week: at Goodman's first lesson he was told to prepare Liszt's vast Prelude and Fugue on a Theme of B.A.C.H. for the following week. Then, when GTB found that his pupil was having difficulty with a trill, he commented: 'You must cultivate a good trill, Peter,' but he offered no further guidance. Another pupil, Alan Willmore, made the mistake of coming to a lesson prepared to play a piece which he had performed the previous week. GTB protested: 'We discussed this last time.' 'Yes, but I've been practising the points you raised, and can now play it much better.' 'Well, in that case,' replied GTB, 'let's hear something else.' Margaret Cobb felt that 'one learnt more from watching him play than from what he actually said'. And she is grateful that he never imposed his own ideas: 'One appreciated the opportunity of thinking out one's own interpretations – a habit which has stood one in very good stead as a recitalist.'

However, he never allowed the slightest imperfection. His own rigorous standards as a performer were reflected in his stringent insistence on firm fingers, rock-steady rhythm and no body movement. Kenneth Abbott contrasts this approach with that of two of GTB's regular deputies at the Royal College – Arnold Goldsborough, who was more 'pianistic' and almost encouraged physical gestures, and 'Ossie' Peasgood, who was altogether more easy-going. Paul Murray recalls Thalben-Ball pacing the floor and 'grunting at the slightest possible slip' or muttering 'rhythm' in his ear. Murray and a fellow pupil, Dennis Vaughan, agreed: 'We could play much better when GTB wasn't around because nothing escaped his attention.' And indeed, only a few pupils were able to endure the pressure. Kenneth Abbott, though, recalls the immense satisfaction he felt after he had played Dupré's Prelude and Fugue in G minor at a college concert, and his teacher told him: 'Very fine performance.' It was rare to feel that one had satisfied the Doctor's high expectations.

Paul Murray learned another art from Thalben-Ball: that of improvisation. He was made to harmonise scales (including chromatic scales) in both the right and the left hand, then play simple canons in two and three parts. Finally he learned to embellish a tune in a variety of ways. Throughout this training GTB 'continually referred to the methods employed by the French school of Dupré and colleagues'.

18

'SING WITH YOUR EARS'

Thalben-Ball completed forty years at the Temple in 1959, and to mark the occasion the Inner Temple invited him to become an Honorary Master of the Bench (of whom there can be only five at one time), thus making him the first organist to become a bencher. The Bench Table Orders – lists of the benchers in order of seniority, which govern the seating plan in hall – are regularly revised, and have seen the name of Master Thalben-Ball gradually rising, until after more than twenty years it appears above those of many distinguished judges.

More honours have been rained on him since then: Fellowship of the Royal School of Church Music in 1963; a CBE in the 1967 New Year's Honours list; Fellowship of the Royal Society of Arts and an Honorary D Mus from the University of Birmingham in 1972; Honorary Membership of the Royal Academy of Music (Hon RAM) and Vice-Presidency of The Organ Club in 1973; and an Honorary Fellowship of the Royal Canadian College of Organists in 1977.

Since the war Thalben-Ball had continued to work for the BBC. For ten years he collaborated with Eric Fenn in a Sunday evening Home Service programme of hymns, *Think on These Things*. Fenn would comment, GTB played the piano, and two singers, René Soames and Margaret Godley, performed with him. He continued to direct the BBC Singers and the Daily Service, and he even appeared on television in its early days. The *News of the World* summarised the event: 'The Astaire-like footwork of George Thalben-Ball in his organ recital was a fascinating spectacle. In his breezy manner he told us what we didn't know about the mighty pipe organ, proving himself almost as good an entertainer as that wag at the piano, Gerald Moore.'

His final broadcast of evensong before his official retirement from

The presentation by EMI of gold discs to Ernest Lough and GTB marked the sale of over a million copies of the Temple choir's recording of Mendelssohn's *Hear my prayer.*

the BBC was transmitted from All Souls', Langham Place, on 9 July 1969.

But he remained in contact with his successor, Barry Rose. Once they met at Broadcasting House in the eighth-floor canteen. GTB, as always, opened the conversation by saying what a good job he thought Barry was doing. But it was not long before he mentioned that certain of his introits were being sung too slowly: 'If the sense of the words is exciting,' he explained, 'one should feel it in the performance of the music.' And when his successor suggested that he was performing the works at the metronome speeds marked, GTB shrugged and said *they* must be too slow. Since then, roughly a third of his introits have been replaced by new pieces composed by Grayston Ives. Rose has great respect, he says, for the remainder: 'They never wear thin, however many times you do them'; and he adds: 'GTB has a rare feeling for the words.'

Just once since he retired, GTB has been asked back to direct a Daily Service. Barry Rose was on holiday in Sussex, listening to the broadcast in bed. He was thrilled by Thalben-Ball's psalm

Three virtuoso organists in conversation: *left to right*, the Italian maestro Fernando Germani with Simon Preston and GTB at the house of Colin Goulden in 1962.

accompaniment until, for two verses, he left the choir unaccompanied. Most unusually, the BBC Singers dropped a quarter-tone in pitch. At the beginning of the next verse Rose was all but blown out of bed as almost full organ crashed to the rescue.

When he first took over, Rose was constantly told by the choir: 'The Doctor used to do it like this.' Now it has become a standing joke that if a question of interpretation is raised, someone will take the comparison a stage further and say: 'Of course, in Walford's day, you know, we did it this way.'

David Lewer, in his monumental book on the Temple Church, *A Spiritual Song*, looks back to his own days as a Temple chorister in the early 1930s; Thalben-Ball, he says, 'had the gift of inspiring loyalty and devotion to the high standards of the choir without methods of coercion; the worst punishment was to be sent out of the practice-room . . . But after an apology the matter was soon forgotten; there was never any sarcasm . . . our learning was mostly by example.'

And this is the way Temple choir practices still function: they are

'Doctor' taking choristers' rehearsal, 1977, in the Temple Church.

quiet, unhurried and hard-working; very professional, in fact. The Boys call GTB 'Doctor', they raise their hands when they make a mistake in rehearsal, and they treat him rather as they would a benevolent grandfather, though with no consequent lack of respect. At the rehearsal for a broadcast of evensong from the Temple, Barry Rose was put in his place when he called through the intercom: 'George, is that all right?' The voice of the head chorister replied firmly: 'DOCTOR is upstairs in the organ loft.'

At full practice, GTB sits in front of a small upright piano between the choir stalls. Every so often he will punctuate his directions and criticisms with 'Pretty good', or perhaps 'Jolly good . . . very nice singing . . . *rather* firm . . .'; it's all a question of quiet encouragement, and the choir responds now as it has done for so many years. If GTB does become cross, he is likely to say no more than: 'Oh well, we'll obviously not be able to *do* this. We'll have to do something easier.' When he coaches solo boys, whom he likes to begin as soloists as early in their choir career as possible, he will guide them gently: 'Keep your chest up . . . every note's a *growing* note . . . fatten the sound on those top notes . . . don't strain . . .' And at any sign of bad intonation: 'Don't sing with your voice, sing with your ears.' If in a practice a boy is not ready for a 'lead', he will tell him it's like arriving at Victoria station at 1.16 to catch the 1.16 train. 'If you did that, you would miss it. You must be there ahead.' When he conducts an unaccompanied anthem he uses small gestures, just slight inflexions of his hands and face; and he virtually 'tunes the choir with his eyebrows' (a picturesque phrase of the Reader of the Temple and former colleague of Thalben-Ball at the BBC, Prebendary Kennedy-Bell). Results from the choir are obtained in the same way as they have been from organ pupils: through constant quiet insistence on perfection. Choirmen as well as choirboys will admit after a couple of years in the choir that their singing has improved and their musicianship increased, though they cannot pinpoint any one moment at which a change took place.

Playing the piano, conducting the choir and making encouraging comments: GTB in action at a rehearsal.

Dr Thalben-Ball is not a teacher in the accepted, formal sense, but he exerts an important influence over those with whom he comes into contact, whether choristers, organ pupils or simply admirers. Many choristers particularly remember occasions when they were allowed into the organ loft to sit by 'Doctor' for a service. It would be quite in character for GTB to turn to a boy after, say, the introit, and ask: 'What did you think of that?' Whatever the answer, the child's pride in having been asked would boost his morale and result in great loyalty to both choirmaster and choir, while GTB's encouragement of constructive criticism in his choristers has led to a more intelligent approach by them to music and to singing.

Michael James was head chorister at the Temple and is now a fine organ recitalist. 'Doctor never gave me an organ lesson as such,' he says, 'but he formed my understanding of the instrument.'

Visitors who have come thousands of miles to meet the great Doctor are sometimes surprised to find such a mild man, worrying about the latest breaking voice in the choir, or telling a chorister to eat some biscuits before he goes home, because he has such a long journey. When, in 1977, he visited Canada and gave a recital in St Matthew's, Ottawa, he insisted on first meeting the church choir, which was to sing a motet between the two halves of his programme. He wished the boys luck, and asked the head chorister to come and see him afterwards. Much to their delight, he had bought the lads four pounds of chocolates as a surprise.

Not long ago, after Temple full practice on a Friday evening, a chorister came out of the church into the lobby where GTB was standing talking: 'Doctor, there's a ghost in the church.' 'Oh really? I suppose you want me to come and have a look?' He grinned good-naturedly as the boy led him into the church. The lad had discovered that if he put his right foot on the piano's sustaining pedal and depressed the soft pedal quickly a few times with his left foot, a series of notes would play by themselves in a ghost-like sort of way. GTB laughed and got him to do it again. Then he said: 'But y'know, there aren't any ghosts here'; and proceeded to tell three stories of supernatural happenings which he had witnessed in the church – the time something grabbed him by the neck from behind in the dark; the time rows of hymn books were thrown to the floor with a loud crash, but were back in their places by the time he had climbed down from the organ loft to

In the Inner Temple, where GTB has lived since his wife died in 1961. He is seen soon after moving in, with his brother Sydney, Sydney's wife Pauline and their son Adrian. The trees in the background hide the Embankment and the River Thames.

investigate; and the time of the mysterious loud knockings on the door when nobody was outside. 'But there are no ghosts *here*,' he repeated to the wide-eyed choristers.

Thalben-Ball is no newcomer to such happenings. Surprisingly, Garrick House, on the site of the former theatre on Richmond Green, in which he lived with his family before the war, did not appear to be haunted. But in their next house, a big building in the Ridgeway, Wimbledon, footsteps were frequently heard on the stairs and in the passages. They usually started from the flat upstairs (originally the servants' quarters) and proceeded downstairs and out of the house. One night GTB, his wife and his daughter heard the descent (though his son John slept through it), and the loud slamming of a door below; on investigation all the doors were found to be locked and bolted, just as they had been left. On another occasion, though, John heard thumps and shouted: 'Is anybody there?' He went downstairs to discover that he had frightened away an all-too-real cat burglar.

GTB was married to Evelyn for thirty-five years. 'An angel

July 31—Eighth Sunday after Trinity

8.30 a.m.   HOLY COMMUNION

11.15 a.m.   MORNING PRAYER

Before the Service—

The Lord God Omnipotent reigneth. Let us rejoice and be glad and give honour unto him. Alleluia.

Psalms 146, 148, 150

1ST LESSON: Ecclesiasticus 17, 1–14

*Te Deum Laundamus—*Stanford in C

2ND LESSON: St. Mark 10, 35–45

*Jubilate Deo—*Davies in G (Festal)

Anthem

Aria S.—Laudamus te, benedicimus te,
adoramus te, glorificamus te.
Full—   Gratias agimus tibi propter magnam gloriam tuam.
(J. S. Bach)

Hymns 372, 311

*Preacher—*The Master

Vox ultima Crucis

Tarry no longer, towards thine heritage
Haste on thy way and be of right good cheer.
Go each day onward on thy pilgrimage.
Think how short time thou shalt abide thee here.
Thy place is built above the starres clear;
None earthly palace wrought in so stately wise.
Come on my friend, my brother most dear!
For thee I off'red my blood in sacrifice.
Tarry no longer!   (John Lydgate)

*Organ Voluntary—*Fugue in E flat (St. Anne)—J. S. Bach

———

There will be no Services during August and September. Services will be resumed on Sunday, October 2, 1977

**By Order of the Choir Committee
G. T. THALBEN-BALL,
Organist and Director of the Choir.**

The final Sunday morning service of the year, on 31 July 1977. Choral mattins is sung each week at 11.15, and congregations are attracted to the unique combination of traditional language, fine music, first-class preaching and minimal ceremonial. Most worshippers stay to listen to the final organ voluntary.

walked on earth', reads the inscription on her tombstone in High-gate cemetery. And indeed, following her death in 1961, after years of suffering from angina, her husband could no longer bear to live in the same house. When he was offered a flat in Paper Buildings, within the Inner Temple, he was grateful to move there. What is more, he claims the seventy-four steps he must climb to reach this flat have helped him to remain in good health.

Good health, with the exception of a serious illness in 1967. He was operated on twice, and it was generally predicted that he would not recover. At the Temple, services were played by several dis-tinguished deputies, including Harold Darke, Sir William McKie and Martin Neary. And the contrast between Darke and McKie was marked. Darke favoured slower tempi than GTB, and tried to alter the choir's style of singing. Sir William, however, character-istically diplomatic in his dealings with a choir devoted to its regular choirmaster, made it clear that he would respect 'the Temple way' while he was in charge. One of the choristers summarised the change dramatically in his diary when he wrote: 'Out of the Darke ages, into the victory of Sir William!' Sir William himself was particularly impressed with the efficiency of the head chorister, who came to the loft after each service to hear the organist's verdict on the singing. The other boys remained robed until the pronounce-ment had been conveyed to them. What amused Sir William was that this particular head chorister first reported to the others: 'Sir William says . . .', but followed this with: 'And *I* think . . .' – another tribute to GTB's encouragement of self-criticism, rather than any untoward reflection on the boy.

Against all predictions GTB not only recovered fully, but the day after his second operation was sitting up in bed doing five-finger exercises and discussing the programme for a recital he was due to give in a month's time. And the following year he was well enough to marry a second time, though sadly this union was not a success and was annulled four years later.

On a happier note, an American lady was introduced to Thalben-Ball after a Temple service. 'Oh, you're the organist? I *dote* on music,' she informed him. 'Really? Yes, well, who's your favourite composer?' he asked. 'My favourite composer', she replied, 'is Wagner.' 'And your favourite opera?' 'I like *Tristan and Isolde* best, and *Oberammergau* a good second.'

19

LOOKING AHEAD

Thalben-Ball is a fine story-teller. Whether all the details are entirely unembellished is open to question, but their timing is impeccable. One of his favourites concerns the occasion he was invited by the mayor and corporation of Westcliff-on-Sea to attend the opening by Gracie Fields of a new cinema. When he arrived he was asked if he would play the National Anthem at the beginning of the ceremony. 'Not having played a cinema organ before,' he continues, 'I asked the regular organist whether it had a drum roll I could use to begin the anthem. "O yes," he told me. "If you press that pedal, there will be a splendid drum roll." But he didn't tell me that if I pressed the pedal too firmly, something quite different would happen. Well, I pressed the pedal in a businesslike way – and all the effects department of the organ started to perform! The National Anthem began with bicycle bells, motor horns and (very loudly from one side of the room) voices calling "Cuckoo! Cuckoo!" I can still see Gracie Fields looking down at me in amazement.'

Then there was the time he played for a Roman Catholic mass, for which the priest had written out all the music on three sheets of manuscript paper. GTB was to play each item in turn when the priest nodded his head. But the priest bobbed and wove so much that GTB went three times through the entire cycle.

Even more disconcerting was the time he stayed with a parson in a village in Anglesey and was asked by him to play the organ for a service. 'It was a harmonium with the stool attached to it, and in a very bad state of repair. So I spent the previous evening oiling and cleaning it; but I apparently overdid the oiling. The moment I began to play the first hymn the whole contraption started to move across the chancel. I tried to back-pedal, but it was no good, and I ended up against the opposite wall, still pumping with my feet.'

A National Anthem...
with Bells on

GTB with his friendly rival of old, Harold Darke, and former Prime Minister, the Right Honourable Edward Heath, at The Organ Club's annual luncheon in 1975, the year in which Thalben-Ball was made a Vice-President of the Club. They are watched by John S. Smith, President of the Club in 1977–8.

GTB was invited in 1975 to give the last of six inaugural recitals on the new Rodgers electronic organ in the Carnegie Hall, New York – and he was flown across the Atlantic first of all for a practice session and later for the recital itself! He played music which he thought Americans would be unlikely to know (by Parry, Camidge, Boyce, J. Bernhard and C. P. E. Bach, Liszt, Mathias, Weitz and himself), but the Parry Fantasia and Fugue in G was not as well received as he had hoped. Neither was GTB terribly impressed with the organ, even though he had had sessions beforehand to try to revoice certain ranks. He found the reeds too similar to one another in texture – 'all *trompeta*-things' – though they had been voiced in consultation with Virgil Fox.

Thalben-Ball has not yet heard an electronic organ to equal the best pipe organ, though he has been impressed by some of the Allen 'computer' instruments. He heard one at the Allen headquarters in Allentown, where 'the tubas might have been Father

Willis'. And in Pittsburgh he preferred the Allen ranks of an organ which also contained conventional pipework by Möller. The instrument temporarily installed in Chichester Cathedral, which had the advantage of a large number of speakers and an excellent acoustic, appealed to him, as did the many possibilities afforded by the Allen installed in 1977 in the Alexandra Palace: he particularly liked the bell effect which he was able to concoct for the end of Wesley's *Holsworthy Church Bells*.

The point is that he feels any new development should be approached with an open mind, and should certainly not be rejected

Talking to the composer Sir Lennox Berkeley during the Jubilee celebrations of The Organ Club in 1976.

out of hand. He tried to show the same sense of fairness in judging cinema organs between the wars. But, as Margaret Cobb put it, 'the outstanding feature of his music is the way that the mechanics of the organ are always subservient to the music. He has the talent for finding the best and most musical effects of *any* instrument.'

And he will take immense trouble to obtain exactly the sound he wants. At St John's College, Cambridge, in 1975, he felt that the *cymbelstern* was a little too loud, and asked Frank Fowler, of Hill Norman & Beard, to soften it. Fowler looked around and saw the cassock belonging to the college organist, Dr George Guest. He held this in front of the offending bells. 'Still not quite distant enough,' said GTB, and asked if Fowler would hold up two cassocks rather than one. And this is exactly what was done at that evening's recital.

Thalben-Ball's approach is practical. Thus in Ottawa in 1977, after listening to a recital on a new two-manual 'classical' Casavant organ, he was heard with the American organist Searle Wright discussing the advantages of interchanging black and white keys. He considered a white C natural and a black C sharp the more desirable because in this arrangement the gaps between the keys were more visible, and the player was therefore more likely to play accurately. And he could see no point in having the stop knobs drawn at right angles to the right and left of the manuals, since it simply caused inconvenience to the player – as must a lack of pistons and other accessories. He could not understand why a builder should wish to make an organist's job any more difficult than it is already.

Before the 1977 rebuild of the St Paul's Cathedral organ, Dean Sullivan asked Thalben-Ball where he thought would be the best position for the new console. 'In your stall,' replied GTB, who considered that only from that position would it be possible for the player to hear the various departments of the organ with equal clarity. He considered that to move the console from inside the north case to a position over the south choir stalls was, if anything, a retrograde step. However, this is what was done, and at GTB's recital (one of the opening series) he was given a standing ovation for his handling of the instrument and of the cathedral's notorious acoustic. He had been particularly worried about co-ordination, in a piece by John Stanley, between the solo melody (played on the new royal trumpet rank in the west end) and the accompaniment (from the dome). The performance was both precise and stunning in its effect.

When the death of Dorothy Howells was announced in 1975, GTB asked her husband Herbert if he might borrow a copy of his tune *Chosen*. This piece had been inspired by the unrivalled view of the Malvern Hills from the top of Chosen Hill. Dorothy had once told her husband, as they stood there together, that he should compose a tune to equal the beauty of the view. He did, and the piece for violin and piano was widely played between the wars. However, Howells was unable to find a copy in 1975, and since the

Deep in conversation with Sir William McKie during GTB's 1977 visit to Canada. Sir William, like GTB, was born in Australia, but after retiring as organist of Westminster Abbey he settled in Canada. The two are seen in Ottawa, at the home of John Springford, British Council representative in Canada.

piece had long been out of print he wrote it out from memory. During the funeral service GTB wove an improvisation around it, just as he had improvised around a number of short pieces at the couple's wedding. Howells was deeply touched by the gesture.

Thalben-Ball's energy is remarkable. His hectic North American tour in 1976 (when he caught up on sleep in Miami by settling down in the archbishop's throne in the sanctuary of the cathedral, and so avoided one of the many exhausting receptions); his Canadian tour in 1977; his weekly visits to Birmingham; his regular choir practices and services at the Temple; his other recitals throughout Britain: he seems to flourish on all these activities. Ralph Downes attended a special recital at St Michael's, Cornhill, and as he approached the entrance he saw Harold Darke (who had by then been succeeded as organist by Richard Popplewell) being helped up the stairs by 'a debonair young man'. As Downes caught up with them he realised that the 'young man' was GTB.

As the years go by GTB's playing, his musicianship and his choir training remain unsurpassed. Howells heard his own *Te Deum (Collegium Regale)* recently at the Temple and commented: 'It was so beautifully done. There is no accompanying like George's.'

And he continues to learn and perform new music: he has recorded Noel Tredinnick's *Brief Encounters*, dedicated to GTB 'in admiration' in 1976; and the recital of choral and organ music given in March 1979 in the Temple Church in celebration of his sixty years there included the first public performance of the specially commissioned *Kerygma* by Malcolm Williamson. But he holds strong views about contemporary musical developments. Sitting at the organ he will play a few random clusters, then cover the keyboard with his arms. 'In some pieces that goes on for twenty-five minutes. It's not really music at all; I don't know why the BBC broadcasts it.' In judging a new work he insists that there be two essentials: 'There must be some kind of line or slope – I won't say necessarily melody – and there must be a pulse or rhythm, so that the music goes somewhere. Harmonic colour is important as well. Messiaen', he continues, 'uses as much dissonance as anyone, but the chords are laid out so that they can sound beautiful.

GTB in his beloved Temple Church.

You know, even cows mooing together in a field can make an enjoyable sound, but sounds in music have to be organised sensibly, with balance.' When he has time GTB likes to listen to local radio 'phone-in' programmes, but the signature tune on the London station LBC annoys him: its repetitiveness he finds typical of much weak modern composition. 'Music mustn't become static. There must be movement and development.'

And that nicely sums up George Thalben-Ball and his outlook on everything he undertakes. He is moving, just as is the music he champions. He dislikes music to be in a rut, just as he would hate to fall into one himself. He looks to the future, to new ideas and fresh plans.

Appendix I:

DISCOGRAPHY

B3855 (HMV 10in)	*Holsworthy Church Bells* (Wesley), *Bridal March* from *Lohengrin* (Wagner): Alexandra Palace
B4484 (HMV 10in, four sides)	*Peer Gynt Suite no 1* (Grieg): Kingsway Hall
B8094 (HMV 10in)	*Wedding March* (Mendelssohn), *War March of the Priests* (Mendelssohn): BBC Concert Hall
B8127 (HMV 10in)	*Toccata in F* (J. S. Bach): BBC Concert Hall
C1458 (HMV 12in)	*Nun danket* (Karg-Elert), *Largo* (Handel): Temple Church
C2038 (HMV 12in)	*Finlandia* (Sibelius): Alexandra Palace
C2209 (HMV 12in)	*Grand March* from *Tannhäuser* (Wagner), *Ride of the Valkyries* from *Die Walküre* (Wagner): Alexandra Palace
HQM 1199 & HLM 7065 (EMI LPs)	Reissue of C2209 and B3855, together with recordings by Alcock, Cunningham, Dupré and R. Goss-Custard, entitled *The Alexandra Palace Organ*
Polydor Select 2460 243	*Trumpet Tune* (Stanley, arr GTB), *Minuet in D* (Stanley, arr GTB), *Gavotte* (Camidge), *Holsworthy Church Bells* (Wesley), *Largo, Allegro, Aria and Two Variations* (Festing, arr GTB), *Fantasia and Fugue in C minor* (C. P. E. Bach),

	Grand Choeur Dialogue (Gigout), *Rondeau, 'La Musette'* (Dandrieu, arr GTB), *Dankpsalm* (Reger), *Prelude on 'Picardy'* (Joubert), *Fiat Lux* (Dubois): Allen computer organ in Chichester Cathedral
PES 5280/7EP 7126 (EMI EP)	*Air* from *Berenice* (Handel), *Fantasia in C* (Bach, arr Keller), *Trumpet Tune* (Stanley), *Voluntary on the Old Hundredth* (Purcell), *Trumpet Voluntary* (Clarke): Temple Church
VPS 1046 (Vista LP)	*Fanfare for Organ* (Cook), *Tune in E* (GTB), *Brief Encounters* (Tredinnick), *In Paradisum* (De Monfred), *Toccata* (Creston), *Sonata on the Ninety-fourth Psalm* (Reubke): All Souls', Langham Place
SEOM 4	*Voluntary on the Old Hundredth* (Purcell): one of a collection of ten pieces played by ten organists at ten venues, entitled *The King of Instruments*. This is the same recording of this piece as on PES 5280/7EP 7126 above
VPS 1059 (Vista LP)	*Toccata, 'Vom Himmel Hoch'* (Edmundson), *Elegy* (GTB), *Interlude in C* (Walford Davies), *Tuba Tune* (Lang), *Variations on a Theme by Paganini* (GTB), *Toccata, Beorma and Poema* (GTB), *Sketch in C, opus 58, no 2* (Schumann), *A stronghold sure* (Bach, arr Grace), *Chorale-Improvisation, opus 65, no 5* (Karg-Elert), *Stella Maris* (Weitz): Temple Church; Birmingham Town Hall; All Souls', Langham Place

RECORDINGS OF THE CHOIR OF THE TEMPLE CHURCH,
DIRECTED/ACCOMPANIED BY GTB

B2493 (HMV 10in)	*O filii et filiae* (arr Walford Davies), *Lift up your hearts* (GTB), *King of Glory* (WD)

B2615 (HMV 10in)   *For all the saints* (Vaughan Williams), *Mine eyes have seen the glory* (WD)

B2627 (HMV 10in)   *Hear ye, Israel*, from *Elijah* (Mendelssohn) (soloist: Ernest Lough)

B2656 (HMV 10in)   *I know that my redeemer liveth*, from *Messiah* (Handel) (soloist: Ernest Lough)

B3047 (HMV 10in)   *Praise my soul* (Goss), *O worship the King* (arr GTB)

B3288 (HMV 10in)   *The Heavens are telling*, from *The Creation* (Haydn)

B3453 (HMV 10in)   *How lovely is Thy dwelling place*, from *German Requiem* (Brahms)

B3518 (HMV 10in)   *How lovely are the messengers* (Mendelssohn), *Lord, it belongs not to my care* (WD)

B3976 (HMV 10in)   *Lullay my liking* (Terry), *There is no rose* (GTB), *Christmas Lullaby* (arr GTB), *See amid the winter's snow* (Goss) (soloist: Denis Barthel)

B4107 (HMV 10in)   *He was despised*, from *Messiah* (Handel), *Alleluia* (Easter Hymn, arr Bridge) (soloist: Denis Barthel)

B4285 (HMV 10in)   *Jerusalem* (Parry), *O little town of Bethlehem* (WD) (soloist: Denis Barthel)

B4364 (HMV 10in)   *Psalm 150* (Franck), *Turn back, O man* (Holst)

B8123 (HMV 10in)   *Lord God of Heaven* (Spohr), *Jesu, joy of man's desiring* (Bach) (oboe: Léon Goossens)

B8380 (HMV 10in)   *As pants the hart* (Spohr), *Blest are the departed* (Spohr)

C1329 (HMV 12in)   *Hear my prayer* (Mendelssohn) (soloist: Ernest Lough)

C1398 (HMV 12in)	*I waited for the Lord* (Mendelssohn), *O come everyone that thirsteth* (Mendelssohn) (soloists: Ernest Lough, Ronald Mallett)
C1436 (HMV 12in)	*Praise the Lord, O my soul* (Wesley)
C1541 (HMV 12in)	*Blessed be the God and Father* (Wesley)
C1878 (HMV 12in)	*Hallelujah* (Beethoven), *Saint Patrick's Prayer* (Burke)
C2053 (HMV 12in)	*Insanae et vanae curae* (Haydn)
7EG8293 (EMI EP)	Reissue of C1329 and B2656
7P111 (EMI EP)	Reissue of C1329
7EG8320 (EMI EP)	Reissue of B3047 and items from B2493 (WD) and B2615, entitled *Hymns we love*
7EG8679 (EMI EP)	Reissue of B2627 and one item from C1398 (*I waited for the Lord*)
CSD 1281/CLP 1309 *Christmas Carols*	*Hark! the herald angels sing* (Wesley–Mendelssohn, arr Cummings), *What sweeter music* (Robert Herrick), *God rest you merry, gentlemen* (trad, arr Chambers), *Gabriel's Message* (Gould–Basque carol), *O Child most holy* (Durrant), *While shepherds watched* (trad, arr WD), *Come let us unite* (Bedell), *Angels from the realms of glory* (Montgomery–Williams), *Three Kings* (Cornelius), *Unto us a Boy is born* (Dearmer–Shaw), *Christ was born on Christmas Day* (trad, arr WD), *Away in a manger* (arr GTB), *In dulci jubilo* (Pearsall, arr Westbrook), *The Holly and the Ivy* (trad, arr WD), *Shepherds in the Field* (trad, arr Wood), *The first Nowell* (arr WD), *O come, all ye faithful* (arr Chambers), *Sing Heaven imperial* (William Dunbar), *Gloria in excelsis Deo* (GTB) (speaker: Richard Brown; soloist: Robin Lough)

CSD 1364/CLP 1452
Favourite Hymns and Organ Voluntaries from the Temple Church

Voluntary on the Old Hundredth (Purcell)*, *All people that on earth do dwell* (Old Hundredth), *Dear Lord and Father* (Repton), *O praise ye the Lord* (Laudate Dominum), *The Lord's my shepherd* (Crimond), *Hark, what a sound* (Highwood), *Love divine* (Love Divine), *God be in my head* (WD), *Solemn Melody* (WD)*, *Fantasia in C* (Bach, arr Keller)*, *Jesus, blessed Saviour* (Eudoxia), *For the beauty of the earth* (Lucerna Laudoniae), *All hail the pow'r* (Ladywell), *The day Thou gavest* (Saint Clement), *My spirit longs for Thee* (Maria Jung und Zart), *O worship the King* (Hanover), *Now thank we all our God* (Nun Danket), *Trumpet Voluntary* (Clarke)*
(soloists: Ian le Grice, Robin Lough, Ernest Lough)

CSD 1415/CLP 1529
Music of the Service from the Temple Church

Introit: *Blessed are the pure in heart* (WD), *Psalm 23* (chant by Walmisley), *Psalm 121* (chant by WD), *Te Deum in C* (GTB), *Jubilate in G* (WD), Anthem: *Jesu, joy of man's desiring* (Bach, arr GTB), Hymn: *The King of love* (Dominus Regit Me), Hymn: *Soldiers of Christ, arise* (Saint Ethelwald), *Psalm 150* (setting by Stanford), Prelude: *If any man will follow Me* (GTB), *Psalm 24* (chant by GTB), *Magnificat and Nunc Dimittis in C* (GTB), Anthem: *How lovely is Thy dwelling place* (Brahms), Hymn: *Come down, O Love divine* (Down Ampney), Hymn: *Forth in Thy name* (Gibbons Song 34), *Trumpet Tune* (Stanley)*
(oboe soloist. Léon Goossens)

GES 5840/7EG 8710

Extracts from CSD 1281: *O Child most holy, Hark! the herald angels sing, In dulci jubilo, O come, all ye faithful*

* Organ solos by GTB

GES 5808/7EG 8614	*Elegy* (GTB)*, *O taste and see* (Vaughan Williams; soloist: Robin Lough), *The souls of the righteous* (Nares; soloists: Robin Lough, Ian le Grice), *Toccata in B minor* (Gigout)*
RES 4291/7ER 5205 *Léon Goossens at* *the Temple Church*	Léon Goossens (oboe) with GTB (organ): *Jesu, joy of man's desiring* (Bach, arr GTB; with Temple Church choir), *Where'er you walk* from *Semele* (Handel), *Sheep may safely graze* (Bach; with Edward Walker, George Crozier, flutes), *Largo* from *Xerxes* (Handel; with Renata Scheffel-Stein, harp)

OTHER RECORDINGS

B2681 (HMV 10in)	*Hark, hark! the lark* (Schubert), *Who is Sylvia?* (Schubert) (soloist: Ernest Lough; pianist: GTB)
B9995/C4039	Christmas carols (The Templars and GTB)
7EP7021	Reissue of B9995 and C4039

* Organ solos by GTB

Appendix II:

SPECIFICATIONS OF SIX ORGANS CLOSELY CONNECTED WITH GTB

An organist spends many hours each week alone, practising in vast empty halls and churches, often well into the night. Not surprisingly, he develops a close relationship with the gigantic musical machine which he is battling to control – a relationship that works two ways. He prises from the monster all that his musicianship, technique, strength and experience will allow; the organ, in its turn, imposes mechanical and acoustical limitations on the player, so that his performance will, for purely practical reasons, be bound to reflect in part the character of the organ.

Examination of the instruments a particular artist knows best must therefore give some clues to the formation and development of his or her individual playing style.

Of those organs with which Dr Thalben-Ball has been best acquainted, and whose specifications form this appendix, the first in importance must be the original instrument in the Temple Church (spec 1). Using it for more than twenty years in its prime role – that of accompanying – he gained agility in fast *crescendi* and *diminuendi* through use of the Rothwell stop-tabs underneath the manuals: a facility which he adapts to conventional consoles. And he learned from Walford Davies to exploit the church's 'delicate' acoustic in his use of the organ's range of quiet solo stops.

The modern Temple Church organ, a more powerful instrument noted for the blend of its registers and its wide dynamic range, is also arguably at its finest during the conduct of the Anglican liturgy. Dr Thalben-Ball's piston settings are listed, in order to identify certain solo combinations favoured by him, as well as his method of building up swell, great and pedal choruses. This chart will be of particular value to historians in years to come, as well as to admirers now.

The Royal Festival Hall organ (spec 3) is in a very different tradition, and one with which GTB would not naturally be at home. However, by subtle management he has repeatedly drawn from it unexpectedly 'English' sounds – perhaps a tribute more to his skill than to the resources of the instrument.

In more traditionally British mould, the Alexandra Palace organ (spec 4) was recorded by Dr Thalben-Ball during its final years (see Discography), and one can try to imagine the characteristics which prompted Marcel Dupré to pronounce it the finest concert organ in Europe. GTB's repertory of arrangements of orchestral pieces found a sympathetic medium in this instrument.

Finally, two large organs at which he has scored many successes: the grand Royal Albert Hall instrument (spec 5), which has been in GTB's charge since it was rebuilt in 1934; and the 1834 organ on which he gives up to forty recitals each year: that of Birmingham Town Hall, perhaps the finest instrument of its size and period in the Midlands.

SPECIFICATIONS

1. THE OLD TEMPLE CHURCH ORGAN
(in its 1941 state)

Great		Choir	
Double Open Diapason	16	Lieblich Bordun	16
Open Diapason I	8	Open Diapason	8
Open Diapason II	8	Spitz Flöte	8
Open Diapason III	8	Flauto Traverso	8
Aeolian	8	Lieblich Gedact	8
Stopped Diapason	8	Dulciana	8
Wald Flute	8	Echo Dulciana	8
Principal	4	Gemshorn	4
Nason	4	Lieblich Flöte	4
Harmonic Flute	4	Piccolo	2
Fifteenth	2	Basset Horn	8
Mixture	3 rks	Orchestral Oboe	8
Double Trumpet	16		
Horn	8	*Solo*	
Trumpet	8	Harmonic Flute	8
Clarion	4	Harmonic Flute	4

Tuba	8
Orchestral Trumpet	8

Swell

Bourdon	16
Open Diapason (large)	8
Open Diapason (small)	8
Gamba	8
Voix Céleste	8
Salicional	8
Rohr Gedact	8
Rohr Flute	4
Principal	4
Fifteenth	2
Mixture	3 rks
Contra Fagotto	16
Cornopean	8
Horn	8
Oboe	8
Clarinet	8
Clarion	4

Pedal

Sub Bass	32
Major Bass	16
Open Bass	16
Open Diapason	16
Violone	16
Stopped Bass	16
Principal	8
Violoncello	8
Bass Flute	8
Trombone	16
Contra Oboe	16

Accessories

5 composition keys and 5 composition pedals to Great with Pedal.
5 composition keys and 5 composition pedals to Swell.
5 composition keys to Choir, 5 to Solo.
5 'general' composition pedals.
Swell pedals to Swell and Choir.
Reversible pedals operating Swell and Choir Tremulants.
1 reversible pedal operating Great to Pedal coupler.

2. THE MODERN TEMPLE CHURCH ORGAN
(as in 1978)

Great　　　　　　　　　　*(Piston settings: see note)*

Double Geigen	16							
Bourdon	16							
Large Open Diapason	8							
Small Open Diapason	8		3.	4.	5.	6.	7.	8.
Geigen	8	2.	3.	4.	5.	6.	7.	8.
Hohl Flute	8					6.	7.	8.
Stop'd Diapason	8	1.	2.	3.	4.	5.	6.	7.	8.
Octave	4				4.	5.	6.	7.	8.
Wald Flute	4								
Octave Quint	$2\frac{2}{3}$						7.	8.

		1	2	3	4	5	6	7	8
Super Octave	2					5.	6.	7.	8.
Harmonics	18. 20. 22. 23						6.	7.	8.
*Tromba (harmonic)	8								8.
*Octave Tromba (harmonic)	4								8.

(*in Solo box)

Choir (enclosed)

		1	2	3	4	5	6	7	8
Contra Dulciana	16						6.	7.	
Claribel Flute	8	1.	2.	3.	4.			7.	
Lieblich Gedeckt	8			3.	4.				8.
Dulciana	8	1.			4.				
Salicet	4				4.				
Flauto Traverso	4		2.	3.		5.	6.		
Harmonic Piccolo	2			3.				7.	
Dulciana Mixture	15. 19. 22					(5.)	6.		
Cor Anglais	16					5.			
Clarinet	8								8.

Solo (enclosed)

		1	2	3	4	5	6	7	8
Contra Viola	16					5.			
Viole d'Orchestre	8	1.							
Viole Céleste	8	1.							
Harmonic Flute	8	1.	2.	3.	4.				
Concert Flute	4			3.	4.	5.			
Orchestral Hautboy	8								
Double Orchestral Trumpet (harmonic trebles)	16							7.	
Horn (harmonic)	8						6.		
**Tuba (harmonic)	8								8.
Octave					4.			7.	
Sub Octave									
Unison Off								7.	

Swell (enclosed)

		1	2	3	4	5	6	7	8
Quintatön	16								
Open Diapason	8			3.	4.	5.	6.	7.	8.
Stop'd Diapason	8		2.	3.	4.	5.	6.	7.	8.
Echo Salicional	8	1.	2.	3.					
Vox Angelica	8	1.							
Principal	4				4.	5.	6.	7.	8.
Fifteenth	2					5.	6.	7.	8.

Mixture	12. 19. 22. 26. 29				6.		8.
Oboe	8					7.	8.
Double Trumpet	16					7.	8.
Trumpet (harmonic trebles)	8						8.
Clarion (harmonic trebles)	4						8.
Octave		1.	2.			7.	

Pedal

Double Open Wood	32					6.	7.	8.
Sub Bourdon	32				5.	6.	7.	8.
Open Wood	16				5.	6.	7.	8.
Open Diapason	16							
Geigen	16			4.	5.	6.	7.	8.
Bourdon	16	1.	2.	3.	4.	5.	6.	7.	8.
Violone	16			3.				
Dulciana	16	1.	2.	3.				
Octave Wood	8							
Flute	8			4.	5.	6.	7.	8.
Octave Flute	4							
Double Ophicleide	32							8.
**Ophicleide	16						7.	8.
Orchestral Trumpet	16						7.	8.
Bassoon	16							
**Posaune	8						7.	8.

(**in separate box*)

Full complement of couplers and accessories

Note: It has been thought helpful to indicate (to the right of the stop names) Dr Thalben-Ball's standard piston settings on the organ which he has, after all, played more than any other during the past thirty years. He warns, however, that this scheme must not be blindly imitated. No two stops of the same name on different organs sound identical, and therefore piston settings must vary from one instrument to the next. However, bearing in mind that these settings are designed specifically for the 'live' acoustic of the Temple Church, and that they are used mainly for service accompaniment, they do give a guide to the sort of sounds (and particularly the type of great, swell and pedal *crescendo*) preferred by Dr Thalben-Ball.

3. THE ROYAL FESTIVAL HALL ORGAN

(built by Harrison and Harrison, 1954; 4 manuals; 102 speaking stops)

Great					
Principal	16		Octave		4
Gedackt Pommer	16		Wald Flute (conical)		2
Diapason (2 rks in treb)	8		Rauschquint	12.	15
Principal	8		Tertian	17.	19
Flûte Harmonique	8		Mixture	19. 22. 26. 29. 33.	36
Rohr Gedackt	8		Basset Horn		8
Quintflöte	5⅓		Trompette Harmonique		8
Octave	4		Clairon Harmonique		4
Gemshorn	4				
Gedeckt	4		*Positive*		
Quint	2⅔		Principal		8
Octave	2		Gedeckt		8
Blockflöte	2		Quintadena		8
Tierce	1⅗		Octave		4
Mixture	15. 19. 22. 26. 29		Rohr Flute		4
Scharf	26. 29. 33. 36		Quintflöte		2⅔
Cornet	1. 8. 12. 15. 17-mid C		Spitzflute		2
Bombarde	16		Tierce		1⅗
Trumpet	8		Larigot		1⅓
Clarion	4		Carillon	29. 38: 1. 8.	10
			Mixture	15. 19. 22. 26.	29
Choir			Scharf	22. 26. 29. 33.	36
Dulciana	16		Dulzian (in Choir box)		8
Open Wood	8		Trumpet (in Choir box)		8
Stopped Wood	8				
Unda Maris (AA) (2 rks)	8		*Swell*		
Spitz Octave	4		Quintadena		16
Open Flute	4		Diapason		8
Principal	2		Gemshorn		8
Quintflöte	1⅓		Quintadena		8
Octave	1		Viola		8
Sesquialtera	26. 31		Voix Célestes		8
Mixture	29. 33. 36. 40		Principal		4
Cromorne	8		Koppelflöte		4
Schalmei	4		Nazard		2⅔
			Octave		2
Solo			Open Flute		2
Diapason	8		Tierce		1⅗
Rohr Flute	8		Flageolet		1
			Mixture	22. 26. 29.	33

Zimbel	38. 40. 43	Quintadena		8
Hautbois	8	Nazard		$5\frac{1}{3}$
Voix Humaine	8	Superoctave		4
Bombarde	16	Spitzflute		4
Trumpet	8	Open Flute		2
Clarion	4	Septerz		17. 21
		Mixture	12. 15. 19. 22	
Pedal		Sharp Mixture	22. 26. 29	
Principal	32	Bombarde		32
Majorbass	16	Bombarde		16
Principal	16	Dulzian		16
Sub Bass	16	Trumpet		8
Quintadena	16	Cromorne		8
Dulciana	16	Clairon		4
Quintflöte	$10\frac{2}{3}$	Schalmei		4
Octave	8	Kornett		2
Rohrgedeckt	8			

Full complement of couplers and accessories

4.   THE ALEXANDRA PALACE ORGAN
(as rebuilt by Henry Willis III, 1929; 4 manuals; 98 speaking stops)

Great		Trumpet	8
Double Open Diapason	16	Posaune	8
Bourdon	16	Clarion	4
Open Diapason no 1	8		
Open Diapason no 2	8	*Choir*	
Open Diapason no 3	8	Contra Viola	16
Clarabella	8	Viola da Gamba	8
Quint	$5\frac{1}{3}$	Viola Celestes (tenor C)	8
Octave 1	4	Claribel Flute	8
Octave 2	4	Lieblich Gedackt	8
Flute Couverte	4	Dulciana	8
Octave Quint	$2\frac{2}{3}$	Gemshorn	4
Super Octave	2	Viola	4
Seventeenth	$1\frac{3}{5}$	Nason Flute	4
Furniture	2 rks	Nazard	$2\frac{2}{3}$
Sesquialtera	3 rks	Piccolo	2
Mixture	3 rks	Tierce	$1\frac{3}{5}$
Double Trumpet	16	Mixture	3 rks
Trumpet-harmonic	8	Corno-di-Bassetto	8

Cor Anglais	8
Trumpet	8
Clarion	4
Tremulant	

Solo

Violoncello	8
Tibia	8
Viole d'Orchestre	8
Violes Celestes (BB)	8
Flute-harmonique	8
Octave 'Cello	4
Concert Flute	4
Solo Nazard	$2\frac{2}{3}$
Piccolo-harmonique	2
Bassoon	8
Orchestral Oboe	8
Orchestral Clarinet	8
Contra Tromba	16
Tromba-harmonic	8
Tuba-harmonic	8
Clarion-harmonic	4
Tubular Bells (20 notes)	
Tremulant	

Swell

Double Open Diapason	16
Lieblich Bourdon	16
Open Diapason no 1	8
Open Diapason no 2	8
Flute Couverte	8
Rohr Flute	8
Salicional	8
Vox Angelica (tenor C)	8
Principal	4
Flauto Traverso	4
Twelfth	$2\frac{2}{3}$
Fifteenth	2

Furniture	2 rks
Sesquialtera	3 rks
Mixture	3 rks
Waldhorn	16
Cornopean	8
Hautboy	8
Vox Humana	8
Clarion	4
Contra Posaune	16
Trumpet	8
Tremulant	

Pedal

Double Open Bass (ext Open Bass no 2)	32
Double Open Diapason	32
Sub Bass (ext Bourdon)	32
Open Bass no 1	16
Open Bass no 2	16
Contra Basso	16
Bourdon	16
Bass Viola	16
Octave	8
Principal (1)	8
Viola (ext Bass Viola)	8
Flute	8
Super Octave (1)	4
Octave Viola (ext Viola)	4
Octave Flute (ext Flute)	4
Sesquialtera	3 rks
Mixture (2)	3 rks
Bombarde (1)	32
Trombone (1)	16
Ophicleide (2)	16
Clarion (2)	8
Octaves on Pedal Chorus (1)	
Octaves on Pedal Chorus (2)	

Full complement of couplers and accessories

5. THE ROYAL ALBERT HALL ORGAN

(built by Henry Willis, 1871–2; rebuilt by Harrison and Harrison, 1924, 1934, 1973. This is the 1978 specification: 4 manuals, 146 speaking stops)

Great
(first division)

Contra Violone	32
Contra Gamba	16
Double Claribel Flute	16
Open Diapason I	8
Open Diapason III	8
Open Diapason IV	8
Viola da Gamba	8
Rohr Flute	8
Quint	$5\frac{1}{3}$
Principal	4
Viola	4
Harmonic Flute	4
Octave Quint	$2\frac{2}{3}$
Super Octave	2
Harmonics 10. 15. 17. 19. 21.	22
Contra Tromba	16
Tromba	8
Octave Tromba	4
Posaune	8
Harmonic Trumpet	8
Harmonic Clarion	4

Great
(second division)

Double Open Diapason	16
Bourdon	16
Open Diapason II	8
Open Diapason V	8
Geigen	8
Hohl Flute	8
Octave	4
Fifteenth	2
Mixture 8. 12. 15. 19. 22	
Cymbale 19. 22. 26. 29. 31. 33. 36	

Solo and Bombard
(first division: Solo)

Contra Bass	16
Flûte à Pavillon	8
Viole d'Amour	8
Doppel Flute	8
Harmonic Claribel Flute	8
Unda Maris (2 rks)	8
Wald Flute	4
Flauto Traverso	4
Piccolo Traverso	2
Double Bassoon	16
Corno di Bassetto	8
Hautboy	8
Bassoon	8
Double Horn	16
French Horn	8
Carillons (tenor C)	
Tubular Bells (middle C)	
Tremulant	

Solo and Bombard
(second division: Bombard)

Bombardon	16
Tuba	8
Orchestral Trumpet	8
Cornopean	8
Quint Trumpet	$5\frac{1}{3}$
Orchestral Clarion	4
Sesquialtera 12. 15. 17. 19.	22
Contra Tuba	16
Tuba Mirabilis	8
Tuba Clarion	4

Choir and Orchestral
(first division: Choir)

Open Diapason	8
Lieblich Gedeckt	8
Dulciana	8
Gemshorn	4
Lieblich Flute	4
Nazard	$2\frac{2}{3}$
Flageolet	2
Tierce	$1\frac{3}{5}$
Mixture	15. 19. 22
Trumpet	8
Clarion	4

Choir and Orchestral
(Second Division: Orchestral)

Contra Viole	16
Violoncello	8
Viole d'Orchestre I	8
Viole d'Orchestre II	8
Viole Sourdine	8
Violes Celestes (2 rks)	8
Viole Octaviante	4
Cornet de Violes	12. 15. 17. 29. 22
Quintaton	16
Harmonic Flute	8
Concert Flute	4
Harmonic Piccolo	2
Double Clarinet	16
Clarinet	8
Orchestral Hautboy	8
Cor Anglais	8
Tremulant	

Swell

Double Open Diapason	16
Bourdon	16
Open Diapason	8
Viola da Gamba	8
Salicional	8
Vox Angelica	8
Flûte à Cheminée	8
Claribel Flute	8
Principal	4
Viola	4
Harmonic Flute	4
Octave Quint	$2\frac{2}{3}$
Super Octave	2
Harmonic Piccolo	2
Mixture	8. 12. 15. 19. 22
Furniture	15. 19. 22. 26. 29
Contra Oboe	16
Oboe	8
Baryton	16
Vox Humana	8
Double Trumpet	16
Trumpet	8
Clarion	4
Tuba	8
Tuba Clarion	4
Tremulant	

Pedal

Acoustic Bass	64
Double Open Wood	32
Double Open Diapason	32
Contra Violone	32
Double Quint	$21\frac{1}{3}$
Open Wood I	16
Open Wood II	16
Open Diapason I	16
Open Diapason II	16
Violone	16
Sub Bass	16
Salicional	16
Viole (in Choir Box)	16
Quint	$10\frac{2}{3}$
Octave Wood	8
Principal	8
Violoncello	8
Flute	8
Octave Quint	$5\frac{1}{3}$
Super Octave	4

Harmonics	
10. 12. 15. 17. 19. 21. 22	
Mixture (in Solo box)	
15. 19. 22. 26. 29	
Double Ophicleide	32
Double Trombone (in Swell box)	32
Ophicleide	16
Bombard	16
Trombone (in Swell box)	16
Fagotto	16
Trumpet (in Swell box)	16
Clarinet (in Choir box)	16
Bassoon (in Solo box)	16
Quint Trombone	$10\frac{2}{3}$
Posaune	8
Clarion	8
Octave Posaune	4
Bass Drum	

Full complement of couplers and accessories

6. BIRMINGHAM TOWN HALL ORGAN

(built by William Hill, 1834; rebuilt by Henry Willis, 1933; 4 manuals; 90 speaking stops

Great			
Double Open Diapason	16	
Bourdon	16	
Open Diapason no 1	8	
Open Diapason no 2	8	
Open Diapason no 3	8	
Open Diapason no 4	8	
Gamba	8	
Hohl Flute	8	
Octave	4	
Principal	4	
Flute Couverte	4	
Twelfth	$2\frac{2}{3}$	
Fifteenth	2	
Sesquialtera	17. 19. 22	
Mixture	19. 22. 26. 29	
Double Trumpet	16	
Trumpet	8	
Clarion	4	

Choir (enclosed)	
Lieblich Gedackt	16
Open Diapason	8
Viola da Gamba	8
Triangular Flute	8
Stopped Diapason	8
Dulciana	8
Viola	4
Wald Flute	4
Lieblich Flute	4
Nazard	$2\frac{2}{3}$
Piccolo	2
Tierce	$1\frac{3}{5}$
Septieme	$1\frac{1}{7}$
Contra Fagotto	16
Cornopean	8
Cor Anglais	8
Krummhorn	8

Solo (enclosed)	
Violoncello	8
Viole d'Orchestre	8
Violes Celestes (T.C.)	8
Harmonic Flute	8
Rohr Flute	8
Octave Viole	8

Harmonic Flute	4	Trompette	8
Harmonic Piccolo	2	Posaune	8
Clarionet	8	Oboe	8
Orchestral Oboe	8	Clarion	4
Vox Humana	8		
French Horn	8	*Pedal*	
Contra Tromba	16	Double Open Bass	32
Tromba	8	Double Open Diapason	32
Clarion	4	Open Bass no 1	16
		Open Bass no 2	16
Solo (unenclosed)		Open Diapason no 1	16
Tuba Mirabilis	8	Open Diapason no 2	16
		Violone	16
Swell (enclosed)		Bourdon	16
Contra Gamba	16	Gamba	16
Bourdon	16	Principal	8
Open Diapason no 1	8	Violoncello	8
Open Diapason no 2	8	Dolce	8
Claribel Flute	8	Fifteenth	4
Aeoline	8	Mixture 15. 17. 19.	22
Salicional	8	Fagotto	16
Vox Angelica (GG)	8	Tromba	16
Octave	4	Tromba	8
Suabe Flute	4	Tromba	4
Twelfth	$2\frac{2}{3}$	Bombarde	32
Fifteenth	2	Trombone	16
Quint Mixture 19. 22. 26.	29	Clarion	8
Contra Posaune	16		

Full complement of couplers and accessories

Appendix III:

SUMMARY OF IMPORTANT DATES

GEORGE THOMAS THALBEN-BALL, CBE, D MUS, HON D MUS (BIRM), FRCM, FRCO, FRSCM, FRSA, HON RAM, FRCCO

1896 Born at 99 Albion Street, Sydney, NSW, Australia, son of George Charles Ball (aged 44) and Mary Hannah Ball, née Spear (aged 42) (18 June)

1899 Brother Sydney Charles born at Arrallas Mill, Cornwall (18 October)

1911 Entered Royal College of Music on Associated Board exhibition (9 January)

Appointed Assistant Organist, Whitefield's Tabernacle

1913 First public appearance as an organist at Queen's Hall (14 January)

Gained ARCO (Lafontaine prize) (July)

1914 Elected RCM Foundation Scholar (taking effect 4 May)

Awarded Challen and Son gold medal for piano, RCM (Easter term)

Awarded John Hopkinson gold medal for piano, RCM (Easter term)

Début as organ recitalist with two Alexandra Palace recitals (August)

Appointed Organist and Choirmaster, Holy Trinity, Castelnau, Barnes

1915 Gained FRCO (January)

Gained ARCM (piano performance) (April)

Elected RCM Clarke Scholar (May)

Played solo part in Rachmaninov Piano Concerto no 3 at RCM, conducted by Stanford (only previous London performance 1911 with composer as soloist, conducted by Mengelberg) (13 December)

1916 Awarded RCM Director's history essay prize (Easter term)

Appointed Organist and Choirmaster, St James's, Sussex Gardens, Paddington

Awarded Dannreuther Prize, RCM (Midsummer term)

1917   Performance of Walford Davies's *Everyman* with Pinner Choral Society conducted by Harold Darke, piano accompaniment shared by GTB and composer (26 May)

1918   First appearance at RCM concert as an organist (31 January)

Completed his studies at RCM (April)

1919   Appointed Acting Organist, the Temple Church (6 March)

1923   Recital in the opening series, Westminster Cathedral

Appointed Organist, the Temple Church (taking effect Michaelmas term)

1924   Name altered from George Thomas Ball to George Thomas Thalben-Ball (witnessed by Cunningham) (24 January)

Walford Davies's first radio broadcast to schoolchildren, illustrated by Temple choristers (4 April)

1925   Publication of *A little Organ Book* in memory of Parry (died 7 October 1918): one composition by GTB

South African examining tour and recitals (July–October)

1926   Married Grace Evelyn Chapman at St Peter's, Cranley Gardens (4 January)

Elected to the Council, Royal College of Organists

1927   First gramophone record of the Temple Choir (*Hear my prayer*) released

RCO examiner for the first time

Daughter Evelyn Pamela born (3 October)

1929   President, London Society of Organists

1930   A second South African tour (summer)

1931   French trip for Temple choristers (August)

1932   Son John Michael born (11 May)

1933   Opening of BBC Broadcasting House concert hall organ: GTB, Alcock, Cunningham (16 June)

1934   Reopening of Royal Albert Hall organ: GTB, Alcock, Cunningham (23 January)

First performance of Howells's Sonata by GTB at Royal Albert Hall (20 March)

Appointed Curator of the Organ and Organist, Royal Albert Hall (1 July)

1935   Lambeth Doctorate conferred by Archbishop of Canterbury in Inner Temple Hall (27 November)

1936   Accompanied broadcast memorial service for King George V (26 January)

Recital for Les Amis de l'Orgue at Ste Eustache, Paris
1937 Created a Bard of Cornwall (14 August)
First performance of Walford Davies's Interlude in C ('to GTB and all the Templars') in Temple Church (6 December)
1938 Command Concert, Royal Albert Hall, broadcast to the Empire: including GTB, Temple choristers and Templars' Male Voice Choir
1939 City of London School evacuated to Marlborough. Men-only Temple services from 1 October (except school holidays)
1940 GTB's *Temple Psalter* used for first time (16 June)
1941 Sir Walford Davies died (11 March)
Temple Church bombed (10–11 May)
Appointed Musical Adviser to BBC's Religious Broadcasting Department (9 June)
Received Freedom of the City of London (18 September)
1944 Played for Sir Henry Wood's funeral, Hitchin parish church, with BBC Singers and Orchestra (23 October)
1946 President, Incorporated Society of Organists (1946–8)
1948 President, Royal College of Organists (1948–50)
1949 Appointed City Organist, Birmingham (May, backdated to January)
Appointed University Organist, Birmingham (October)
1951 Australian tour (June–September)
Granted Fellowship of the Royal College of Music (10 October)
1953 Granted Honorary Fellowship of the College of St Nicolas (superseded by FRSCM, 1963)
1954 Re-dedication of Temple Church (23 March)
Opening of Royal Festival Hall organ: Downes, Jeans, Richardson, GTB (27 March)
South African tour (summer)
1956 Reopening of Royal Albert Hall organ after renovation: GTB recital (20 March)
United States début in Lewisohn Stadium, New York (27 June)
1958 Re-dedication of the Round Church (7 November)
1959 Appointed Honorary Master of the Bench of the Inner Temple
1961 Wife Grace Evelyn died (13 July)
Retired as a professor of the Royal College of Music (December)
1962 Gold disc awarded by EMI to GTB and Ernest Lough
1963 Granted Fellowship of the Royal School of Church Music at Addington Palace (20 May)
1967 Made a Commander of the British Empire in New Year's Honours list.
Elected President of the BBC Club Organ Society at its in-

augural meeting (12 September)

1968 Married second wife, Jennifer, in Temple Church (marriage annulled 26 June 1972)

GTB opened RCO auction with an organ *Flourish*, and bought a pipe from the old Temple organ (28 September)

1969 Last broadcast evensong (9 July) to mark retirement from BBC (officially 30 June)

1971 Australasian tour (April–May)

1972 Granted Fellowship of the Royal Society of Arts (10 January)

Granted degree of Hon D Mus by the University of Birmingham (December)

1973 Elected Hon RAM (Royal Academy of Music)

Elected Vice-President of The Organ Club (13 February)

1975 Last of six inaugural recitals on new organ in Carnegie Hall, New York (1 April)

1976 Coast-to-coast recital tour of United States and Canada

1977 Played for Harold Darke's memorial service at St Michael's, Cornhill (14 February)

Recitals in Toronto and Ottawa. Granted Fellowship of the Royal Canadian College of Organists (*honoris causa*) in Ottawa (17 September)

1978 800th recital as City Organist at Birmingham Town Hall (1 February) (broadcast 18 November)

1979 One-hour documentary on GTB's career: BBC Radio 4 (6 March)

First of a series of monthly concerts in the Temple Church to celebrate GTB's sixty years in the organ loft (18 March)

Appendix IV:

THE TEMPLE
MUSIC TRUST

For 150 years, the Temple choir has consistently set an example of musical excellence. Until recently the Inner Temple and the Middle Temple paid the full fees of the choristers as day-boys at the City of London School, and the attraction of this musical scholarship was such that the organist was able to select his boys from a large field of candidates. Now, however, changes have occurred; in particular, school fees have increased, and while there is no intention on the part of the Inns to reduce their voluntary contribution towards the cost of the choir, their heavy responsibilities for the wide range of legal education as well as for the maintenance of the church building and the organ make the need for a wider basis of support clear.

In 1979, under the chairmanship of Sir Hugh Wontner, GBE, CVO, the Temple Music Trust launched an appeal for £100,000, to ensure that the musical tradition of the Temple be maintained and developed. The money is needed for payment of choristers' fees and expenses, up to a total of two-thirds; provision of additional sums in the case of boys who are in clear need of further financial assistance; and payments to well qualified boys, as they leave the choir, to assist the continuance of their education.

Patrons of the appeal include the 1979 Treasurers of the Inner Temple and the Middle Temple, the Hon Mr Justice Thesiger and The Hon Mr Justice Graham; The Rt Hon The Lord O'Brien of Lothbury; The Rt Hon Viscount Dilhorne; The Rt Hon The Lord Diplock; The Rt Rev and Rt Hon Gerald Ellison, Bishop of London; and Dr Malcolm Williamson, Master of the Queen's Music.

The Appeal Organiser is Mrs C. T. Norman-Butler, from whom all details may be obtained. She may be contacted at The Temple Music Trust Appeal Office, 7 Ashley Gardens, London SW1P 1QD (telephone 01-828 1468).

INDEX

Alcock, Sir Walter, 45, 58, 74, 77

Alexandra Palace, 18, 21, 33-5, 78-81, 145

Allen, Sir Hugh, 15, 50, 66, 73, 96, 99, 112

American Guild of Organists, 125, 127

Aprahamian, Felix, 10, 80

Ball, Sydney, 9, 18, 19, 20, 139

Bankes, Lord Justice, 55-6, 60, 61

Beecham, Sir Thomas, 66

Birmingham, 8, 15, 18, 22, 35, 112-15, 126, 127, 133, 148

Boult, Sir Adrian, 9, 66, 98, 99, 119

Bridge, Frank, 49

Bridge, Sir Frederick, 25, 45

British Broadcasting Corporation, 70-72, 77, 78, 94-9, 100, 102, 133-5, 148

City of London School, 69, 87, 92, 110

Cunningham, G.D., 15, 18-22, 26, 33-35, 74, 77, 79, 80, 81, 112, 131

Dakers, Lionel, 10, 17, 103

Darke, Dr Harold, 9, 27, 38, 39, 42-6, 50-6, 74, 87, 141, 144, 148

Davies, Fanny, 24, 35

Davies, Sir Walford, 15, 17, 27, 35-8, 42, 43, 45, 46, 50-60, 61, 66, 68, 70-73, 85, 87-9, 92, 94, 96, 100, 109-10

Daymond, Dr Emily, 28, 58

Demessieux, Jeanne, 124

Dixon, Alfred Capel, 106

Dixon, Reginald, 78

Downes, Ralph, 10, 114, 148

Dupré, Marcel, 15, 29, 50, 77, 79, 80, 81, 87, 121, 124, 129, 132

Ellison, the Rt Rev & Rt Hon Gerald, 10, 87

Falkner, Sir Keith, 9, 64-5

Fenn, the Rev Eric, 10, 94, 97, 102, 133

Foort, Reginald, 46, 78, 81

Fox, Douglas, 37, 46

Fox, Virgil, 15, 126-7, 144

Fryer, Herbert, 24

Germani, Fernando, 78, 120, 135

Glentanar, Lord, 108

Goossens, Eugene, 25, 37, 121

Goss-Custard, Reginald, 79-80

Guest, Dr George, 10, 146

Harris, Sir William, 46, 52, 53

Hartvigson, Frits, 24, 121

Holst, Gustav, 15, 66, 84

Holy Trinity, Castelnau, 35-7

Hopkins, Dr E.J., 17, 70, 100-1, 109, 110

Howells, Dr Herbert, 8, 15, 27, 31, 37, 45-6, 49, 58, 60, 66, 73, 75-7, 104, 112, 124, 147-8

Hurford, Peter, 10, 103

Jacob, Dr Gordon, 9, 64-5

Kennedy-Bell, the Rev Preb W.D., 11, 137

Lemare, Edwin, 28-9, 112-13

174

Lewer, David, 8, 109, 135
Ley, Henry, 53, 58
Lough, Ernest, 8, 61-3, 110, 134

Mackenzie, Master Muir, 44, 53
Macpherson, Sandy, 78
Marchal, André, 79, 80, 81
McKie, Sir William, 9, 72, 109, 141, 147

New York, 125-7, 144

Ord, Boris, 27, 48
Organ Club, the, 133, 144, 145
Organ Music Society, the, 75, 78, 80

Parratt, Sir Walter, 15, 26, 27, 28, 32, 50, 57, 66, 117
Parry, Sir Hubert, 15, 28, 31, 42, 44, 45, 46, 58, 74, 144
Peaker, Dr Charles, 11, 116
Peasgood, Dr Osborne, 81, 91, 106, 131
Preston, Simon, 135
Promenade concerts, 81-3, 117, 119

Queen's Hall, 31, 50, 78, 81-2, 117

Rose, Barry, 12, 134-6
Royal Albert Hall, 15, 74-7, 79, 81, 119-20
Royal Canadian College of Organists, 127, 133
Royal College of Music, 21, 23-32, 35, 38, 45, 47, 50, 53, 64-6, 72, 112, 125, 129, 131
Royal College of Organists, 17, 22, 46, 48, 103, 129-31
Royal Festival Hall, 114-16, 118, 126

St Dunstan-in-the-West, 106
St George's Chapel, Windsor, 26, 72
St James's, Muswell Hill, 18-20, 33

St James's, Sussex Gardens, 39-43, 51, 55
St Margaret's, Westminster, 28-9
St Michael's, Cornhill, 39, 42, 44, 50, 74, 87, 148
St Paul's Cathedral, 98, 127, 146-7
St Peter's, Cranley Gardens, 48, 68
Sargent, Sir Malcolm, 119
Sewell, F.A., 26, 28
Sowerby, Leo, 124
Stanford, Sir Charles, 15, 25, 28, 31, 42, 45, 46-7, 53, 58, 66, 74
Stubbs, Harry, 46, 52
Sydney, New South Wales, 13, 17, 122-123

Taylor, Canon Cyril, 12, 96
Taylor, Franklin, 24, 28
Templars' Union, 38, 57, 60, 72, 111
Thalben-Ball, Dr George: own compositions: 31, 46, 57, 71, 81, 85, 98-9, 110, 126, 130, 134, 144; see also Appendix 1
Thalben-Ball, Evelyn (née Chapman), 67-9, 126, 139-40
Thalben-Ball, John, 9, 68, 139
Thalben-Ball, Pamela, 68-9, 139

Vaughan Williams, Ralph, 27, 58, 66, 74, 84, 95, 99

Watson, Dr Sydney, 9, 64-6
Westminster Abbey, 25, 60, 85, 89, 91, 106, 109, 127, 147
Westminster Cathedral, 66, 128
Whitefield's Tabernacle, 23, 29-31
Willcocks, Sir David, 12
Williamson, Dr Malcolm, 12, 13, 148
Williams, the Rev John G., 12, 95, 97, 99
Wood, Dr Charles, 25, 45, 58
Wood, Sir Henry, 15, 81, 83, 117, 121